SHEFFIELD HALLAM UNIVERSITY
LEARNING & IT SERVICES
ADSETTS CENTRE CITY CAMPUS
SHEFFIELD S1 1WB

D1330185

SHEFFIELD HALLAM UNIVERSITY
LEARNING CENTRE
WITHDRAWN FROM STOCK

First published 2011 by order of the Tate Trustees
by Tate Liverpool
Albert Dock, Liverpool L3 4BB
in association with
Tate Publishing, a division of Tate Enterprises Ltd,
Millbank, London SW1P 4RG
www.tate.org.uk/publishing

on the occasion of the exhibition
Alice in Wonderland
at Tate Liverpool
4 November 2011 until 25 January 2012
Curated by Christoph Benjamin Schulz with Gavin
Delahunty, assisted by Eleanor Clayton

Museo di arte moderna e contemporanea
di Trento e Rovereto
25 February until 3 June 2012

Hamburger Kunsthalle
20 June until 30 September 2012

In Association with

Mersey Care **NHS**
NHS Trust

Supported by

With additional support from:
Liverpool and Sefton Health Partnership Limited
Embassy of the Kingdom of the Netherlands
The British Israeli Arts Training Scheme (BI ARTS)
a British Council initiative in partnership with the
Ministry of Foreign Affairs and the Ministry of Culture
and Sport in Israel
Media Partner The Times

© Tate 2011

All rights reserved. No part of this book may be
reprinted or reproduced or utilised in any form or
by any electronic, mechanical or other means, now
known or hereafter invented, including photocopying
and recording, or in any information storage or
retrieval system, without permission in writing from
the publishers

British Library Cataloguing in Publication Data
A catalogue record for this book is available from the
British Library

ISBN 978-1-85437-991-7

Designed by Murray & Sorrell FUEL

Printed by Westerham Press

Front cover: Charles L. Dodgson, *The Broad Walk, Oxford* 1857

Alice
— IN —
Wonderland
Through the Visual Arts

Edited by Gavin Delahunty and Christoph Benjamin Schulz
with assistance from Eleanor Clayton

Tate Publishing

Contents

6   Forewords

8   Down the Rabbit Hole and into the Museum: Alice and the Visual Arts
    Christoph Benjamin Schulz

36   Lewis Carroll and the Victorian Art World
    Edward Wakeling

56   The Universal Dream Child
    Alberto Manguel

81   Between Eating and Loving an *Alicious* Annotated Fairy Tale
    Carol Mavor

120   Time's Manifolds: The Alice Books
    Gillian Beer

179   List of exhibited works

190   Copyright and photography credits

In Collaboration

"Who in the world am I? Ah, that's the great puzzle!"

Mersey Care NHS Trust is delighted to be working with Tate Liverpool on the Alice in Wonderland Exhibition.

Our long established partnership, which recognises the connection between wellbeing and culture, not only extends our imaginations but provides a range of opportunities that is making a real difference to the people in our community. By stimulating different kinds of conversations and experiences, we are moving away from the language of illness towards that of growth, renewal and resilience; shifting the metaphorical landscape and increasing positive mental health and wellbeing for us all.

The story of Alice with its enduring themes, popular with both adults and children, is the perfect vehicle for stimulating a wider conversation with a bigger audience. The topsy turvy world that Alice discovers on falling down the rabbit hole can reflect a life in which we are all challenged to ask "who am I?"

Alan Yates
Chief Executive

Foreword

In recent years, Tate Liverpool's programme of exhibitions and displays has sought to present the expanded influence of art: from the interaction of art and different cultural disciplines as in the popular Collection display series *This is Sculpture* (2008 – 2011) which involved guest curators from such fields as poetry, fashion design and music, to the engagement of art with politics or consumer culture, as seen in *Picasso: Peace and Freedom* (2010) and *Shopping: A Century of Art and Consumer Culture* (2003). The programme attempts to reflect the reality that art does not exist in a vacuum but is part of a broader field of cultural production, which is in turn part of society as a whole. Far from pulling the discipline down from the heights of 'fine art', this approach reveals the true significance and importance of art as a way to understand and experience the world.

Alice in Wonderland: Through the Visual Arts epitomises this philosophy. Charles Dodgson, or Lewis Carroll as he is more widely known, was himself a polymath: a lecturer in mathematics, ordained as a deacon, photographer and, of course, writer, working not in a vacuum but in the context of an extraordinary circle of friends including now world-famous Pre-Raphaelite painters, sculptors and other writers. His novels, *Alice's Adventures in Wonderland* and *Through the Looking Glass*, have gone on to inform and inspire a huge range of artists throughout the twentieth century. From the Surrealists to numerous contemporary artists, they often provided a route to explore some of their primary concerns, such as exile and war or the function and meaning of language, rather than merely responding to them in an illustrative fashion. Consequently, in addition to demonstrating the universal appeal of the novels, the works in this exhibition also tell a story of artistic production during this time and the manifold approaches of artists to their practice and the world at large.

We are firstly most grateful to Christoph Benjamin Schulz and Peter Gorschlüter for conceiving such an original and ambitious exhibition. We would like to thank in particular Christoph Benjamin Schulz for his enduring patience and endless energy in undertaking the impressive task of bringing this idea to reality. We are in debt to Peter Gorschlüter, previously Head of Exhibitions and Displays at Tate Liverpool, for bringing this project to the organisation and enthusiastically supporting its realisation from the outset. At Tate Liverpool, Gavin Delahunty worked closely with Christoph Benjamin Schulz in both developing the exhibition concept and realising the project, introducing his own individual perspective. Additionally we are very grateful for the contributors of this catalogue for their expertise and knowledge. Their advice and time has been invaluable.

The success of any exhibition is dependent on the generosity of the lenders, and we are greatly indebted to all of the lenders to the exhibition who have agreed to part with much valued works for the duration of the show. We would like to thank Edward Wakeling, both a contributor to the catalogue and lender to the exhibition, who has engaged fully with the exhibition from the beginning, generously offering access to both his impressive collection and his encyclopaedic knowledge of Carroll and his work. Special thanks are due to Rick Baker and the Jason Rhoades Estate, who ensured that Rhoades' spirit and aesthetic remains present in the impressive installation. We would also like to mention our gratitude for the assistance of our colleagues at David Zwirner, Frith Street Gallery, Gagosian, Hauser and Wirth, James Cohan Gallery, Lisson Gallery, Marian Goodman Gallery, and Victoria Miro.

As ever, we would like to express our thanks to the team of dedicated staff at Tate Liverpool, particularly Eleanor Clayton, Assistant Curator, who was instrumental in the realisation of the exhibition and worked side by side with Christoph Schulz to search out artists and artworks, collectors and collections, who have in some way been touched by Carroll's extraordinary literary works. We are also grateful to Wendy Lothian for managing the ever-complicated transport of the artworks; Ken Simons and Barry Bentley for efficiently running a complex installation process; Roger Sinek for his technical expertise; and our team of conservators for their knowledge and skill – particularly Charity Fox, paper conservator, for the sheer number of works that she oversaw and advised upon. Furthermore we would like to thank Jemima Pyne, Ian Malone, and Ami Guest for their support in creating this publication; Maria Percival for thoughtfully curating the complex interpretation for the show; and Amy Higgitt and Harriet Cooper for their support.

We are delighted to have as tour partners Museo d'Arte Moderne e Contemporanea di Trento e Rovereto, and Hamburger Kunsthalle, and would like to thank our colleagues in these institutions, in particular Gabriella Belli, Cristian Valsecchi, and Beatrice Avanzi in Rovereto, and Hubertus Gaßner and Annabelle Görgen-Lammers in Hamburg, for their collaboration. We are grateful for the generous support of Liverpool City Council and the National Lottery through Arts Council England. Additional support has been received from Liverpool and Sefton Health Partnership Limited and the Embassy of the Kingdom of the Netherlands. The media partner for the exhibition is The Times and we are delighted to be working with them again.

Last, but certainly not least, we would like to express our sincerest gratitude to Mersey Care NHS Trust for working in association with Tate Liverpool to make possible not only the exhibition, but also a Learning programme that will run alongside, providing a fully accessible experience for the public, from family activity to study days. In addition to this, a city-wide public programme will run across FACT (Foundation for Art and Creative Technology) and the Bluecoat, continuing to emphasise the interdisciplinary appeal of the novels by exploring the impact of Alice on film, book art and narrative practices. As we reach 150 years since the novels were first published we are thrilled to see that their appeal and relevance in the arts and beyond remains as strong as ever.

Christoph Grunenberg   Andrea Nixon
Director   Executive Director

CHRISTOPH BENJAMIN SCHULZ

DOWN THE RABBIT HOLE AND INTO THE MUSEUM:

Alice — AND THE — Visual Arts

The two *Alices* are not books for children; they are the
only books in which we become children…

Virginia Woolf

Charles Lutwidge Dodgson, a.k.a. Lewis Carroll

Charles Lutwidge Dodgson's books about young Alice are in many ways some of the most astonishing publications in literary history. *Alice's Adventures under Ground* – a little book, a relatively short text, just ninety pages in the manuscript – was originally only intended as a private Christmas present never meant for wider readership. However, following its publication in its final version in 1865, under the title *Alice's Adventures in Wonderland*, it became a bestseller that was to cast an enduring spell over children and adults alike, from literary scholars, philosophers and artists to experts in a variety of fields.

The genesis of the book *Alice's Adventures in Wonderland* is no less curious than its literary content and its reception. Its spiritual father, Charles Lutwidge Dodgson, was born in 1832 in Daresbury in the English county of Cheshire. Having attended school in Richmond, then in Rugby, he moved to Oxford in 1850 to study mathematics at Christ Church, later becoming a lecturer in the subject, and taking deacon's orders in 1861. 1856, the year in which he took up his lectureship, was to be one of the most important years in his life. This was the year that he first adopted the pseudonym Lewis Carroll, on the publication of his poem 'Solitude' in the magazine *The Train*.[1] That year Dodgson also bought his first camera – an Ottewill folding box camera, which cost him £15 (p. 24) – and became an avid photographer, taking images of the area around Oxford, its architecture, gardens and parks. He also photographed natural curiosities, devised comical or artistic scenarios, and experimented with photographic tricks such as double exposures (p. 26).[2] It was only in the early 1850s, with the development of the wet collodion method by Gustav Le Gray and its publication by Frederic Scot Archer, that photography had become accessible to keen amateurs. Overall, Dodgson was best known for his portraits of friends, acquaintances and, above all, their children. Two years after his purchase, in 1858, the Photographic Society of London showed four of his prints, portraits and stagings of children at its annual exhibition at the South Kensington Museum. When he finally retired from his hobby in 1880, he left an œuvre of approximately 3,000 images, which may be one of the most comprehensive photographic records of Victorian England. However, without doubt the most important event of 1856 was the fact that he made the acquaintance of a little girl, Alice Pleasance Liddell, daughter of the Dean of Christ Church, Henry George Liddell, and his wife Lorina Hannah. Alice subsequently sat for him, and he never tired of photographing her in new scenarios that he created for her. The first photograph of Alice was taken on 3 June 1856, when Alice was just four, and the last portrays her at the age of eighteen.

Dodgson's friendship with the Dean's children, especially Alice, was to last for some years. It was on 4 July 1862, on a boating trip on the Isis, from Oxford to Godstow, with the sisters Alice, Edith and Lorina, that Dodgson first came up with a story about a little girl called Alice, who dreams her way into a fantastic world, where she grows and shrinks, nearly drowns in a pool of her own tears, meets a white rabbit, a caterpillar on a mushroom and a choleric Queen of Hearts. Alice was so taken with the story about her alter ego that as the day drew

1. It was Edmund Yates, the editor of the magazine, who advised him on his choice of pen name. The first name is derived from *Ludovicus*, a Latinate version of his middle name Lutwidge, and the second name, Carroll, comes from his first name, Charles, as an anglicised version of the Latin *Carolus*.

2. Dodgson often put these pictures into albums, which not only served as a means to store them, but also provided a physical framework within which he could arrange and compose sequences of images for presentation.

to a close she begged Dodgson to write it down for her. In February 1863 he noted in his diary that he had finished a little book with the title *Alice's Adventures under Ground* (p. 66). However, it was to be weeks, and then months, before he had added all the illustrations to the text. Finally, in November 1864, he presented it to Alice with the dedication 'A Christmas Gift to a Dear Child in Memory of a Summer Day'.

From Humble Gift to Remarkable Book

When the decision had been taken to publish the book, Dodgson resolved to revise substantially his original manuscript. He removed some of the private allusions to the domestic life of the Liddell family and significantly extended the text, adding two new chapters, 'Pig and Pepper' and 'A Mad Tea-Party'. *Alice's Adventures in Wonderland* is almost twice as long as *Alice's Adventures under Ground*. Since Dodgson was not confident in his own abilities as an illustrator, he turned to John Tenniel, who was known both for his cartoons for the magazine *Punch* and for his book illustrations. When the first copies of the book arrived from the printers in July 1865, Tenniel noted the poor quality of the print and Dodgson decided that the entire print run of 2000 should be immediately withdrawn from sale; consequently, a new edition was printed and distributed in November of the same year. This decision enlarged considerably the financial burden on Dodgson, who was covering the entire costs of the book's production. In 1869, the same year that Dodgson started work on the sequel *Through the Looking-Glass*,[3] the first official translations of *Alice's Adventures in Wonderland* into French and German were published; a translation into Italian came out in 1872.[4] In the meantime the *Alice* books had achieved such renown that Dodgson approached Alice Liddell with a request to publish the original manuscript as a facsimile, which was distributed in 1886.[5] In 1887 came the People's Edition, a less expensive production aimed at reaching a wider readership, followed by countless even cheaper editions after the author's death. For *The Nursery 'Alice'* of 1890, Dodgson substantially shortened and revised the text for reading aloud to small children.

The Beauty of the Book

Dodgson, the writer, set great store by the design of the text and the aesthetic appearance of his book. His plans detailing precisely the positions of the illustrations in the text (p. 72) demonstrate the meticulous care that he devoted to the design of the finished product. And although Tenniel developed numerous new motifs for the illustrations, drawings in Dodgson's manuscript and surviving studies reveal the extent of his influence on Tenniel (p. 62).[6] Far from being merely decorative additions, embellishments for the text and the book, the illustrations became an integral part of the literary form.[7] Thus the narrative is less a text in the narrow linguistic sense of letters and words connected to form sentences, than a complex text-image compound, in which two different levels are inextricably intertwined in an multi-media narration.[8] This synaesthetic multimediality, whereby images interact with the text – just as the words on

3. In 1869 Dodgson also published a collection of poems, entitled *Phantasmagoria*. *Through the Looking-Glass* was published in 1871 in an edition of 9,000 copies. 1876 saw the publication of the long nonsense poem *The Hunting of the Snark*, illustrated by Henry Holiday; this was followed in 1889 by the novel *Sylvie and Bruno* and in 1893 by *Sylvie and Bruno Concluded*, both illustrated by Harry Furniss – to name only the most important publications.

4. There were also other translations, though it remains unclear whether these were sanctioned by Dodgson or not. On the translations, see Warren Weaver, *ALICE in Many Tongues: The Translations of Alice in Wonderland*, Madison: University of Wisconsin Press, 1964.

5. The manuscript of *Alice's Adventures under Ground* remained in the ownership of Alice Hargreaves (née Liddell) until 1928. On 3 April 1928 it was sold at Sotheby's for £15,400 – at the time a record-breaking price for a manuscript – to the American book-dealer A.W.S. Rosenbach. On the initiative of a group of American businessmen, the manuscript was donated to England in honour of the country's role in the Second World War, and was presented to the British Museum in 1948.

6. Tenniel drew the actual illustrations for the book straight onto wood blocks, which were then cut by the Dalziel brothers (ill.). Thus the well-known drawings are not preparatory drawings, sketches or studies, but executed after the publication. Curiously, Tenniel uses the design of the Alice figure as we know it from the illustrations of Dodgson's work even before the first Alice book had been published on the cover of *Punch* vol. 46 in 1864(fig.).

7. Accordingly, there are barely any detailed textual descriptions of the individual protagonists or settings.

8. Occasionally, in his letters, Dodgson experimented with mannerist writing styles and with encoding his text by replacing individual words with pictograms, mirror-writing or spiral-writing.

our books to the glass, and then they hold up one in the other room.

"How would you like to live in Looking-glass House, Kitty? I wonder if they'd give you milk in there? Perhaps Looking-glass milk isn't good to drink——But oh, Kitty! now we come to the passage. You can just see a little *peep* of the passage in Looking-glass House, if you leave the door of our drawing-room wide open: and it's very like our passage as far as you can see, only you know it may be quite different on beyond. Oh, Kitty! how nice it would be if we could only get through into Looking-glass House! I'm sure it's got, oh! such beautiful things in it! Let's pretend there's a way of getting through into it, somehow, Kitty. Let's pretend the glass has got all soft like gauze, so that we can get through. Why, it's turning into a sort of mist now, I declare! It'll be easy enough to get through——" She was up on the chimney-piece while she said this, though she hardly knew how she had got

there. And certainly the glass *was* beginning to melt away, just like a bright silvery mist.

In another moment Alice was through the

glass, and had jumped lightly down into the Looking-glass room. The very first thing she did was to look whether there was a fire in the

fireplace, and she was quite pleased to find that there was a real one, blazing away as brightly as the one she had left behind. "So I shall be as warm here as I was in the old room," thought Alice: "warmer, in fact, because there'll be no one here to scold me away from the fire. Oh, what fun it'll be, when they see me through the glass in here, and can't get at me!"

Then she began looking about, and noticed that what could be seen from the old room was quite common and uninteresting, but that all the rest was as different as possible. For instance, the pictures on the wall next the fire seemed to be all alive, and the very clock on the chimney-piece (you know you can only see the back of it in the Looking-glass) had got the face of a little old man, and grinned at her.

"They don't keep this room so tidy as the other," Alice thought to herself, as she noticed several of the chessmen down in the hearth among the cinders: but in another moment, with a little "Oh!" of surprise, she was down on her

thought Alice), saying, "She must go by post, as she's got a head on her——" "She must be sent as a message by the telegraph——" "She must draw the train herself the rest of the way——," and so on.

But the gentleman dressed in white paper leaned forwards and whispered in her ear, "Never mind what they all say, my dear, but take a return-ticket every time the train stops."

"Indeed I shan't!" Alice said rather impatiently. "I don't belong to this railway journey at all——I was in a wood just now——and I wish I could get back there!"

"You might make a joke on *that*," said the little voice close to her ear: "something about 'you *would* if you could,' you know."

"Don't tease so," said Alice, looking about in vain to see where the voice came from; "if you're so anxious to have a joke made, why don't you make one yourself?"

The little voice sighed deeply: it was *very* unhappy, evidently, and Alice would have said something pitying to comfort it, "if it would

distinguished novelist—   THE DAILY MIRROR, APRIL 4,

£15,400 FOR "ALICE IN WONDERLAND"

The scene at Sotheby's yesterday during the sale by auction of the manuscript of Lewis Carroll's "Alice's Adventures in Wonderland." It was knocked down to Dr. Rosenbach, the American dealer, for £15,400.

top and bottom left: pages from *Through the Looking Glass*, 1871

bottom right: Press cutting from the Daily Mirror, 4 April 1928, recounting the sale of the original manuscript.

the page connect with the pages of the book – turns the *Alice* books into a *Gesamtkunstwerk* of a particular kind, one in which the intellectual work and the means of book production go hand in hand. This is to say that Dodgson as the instigator of the publication took all the decisions regarding the design and the printing, the choice of paper, the binding and the cover. The publisher Alexander Macmillan was only responsible for the book's marketing and distribution.

In this connection, mention should be made of carefully calculated optical effects that arise as the reader leafs through the book. In *Alice's Adventures in Wonderland* the Cheshire Cat's disappearance is demonstrated as the reader turns the page, to find now only a faint image of the cat in the same position as it had occupied in all its glory on the previous page. In *Through the Looking-Glass* there is a comparable moment when Alice steps through the mirror. It is as though she is stepping through the page of the book into the mirror world, entering on one page and emerging from the mirror again on the next, as the reader turns the page.[9] The very form of the narrative is unusual, with its episodic structure whereby figures encounter each other in chapters that follow on from each other more like a series of unconnected anecdotes. At the same time, the use of dialogue, the conversations between different characters that take up long stretches of the text, suggests an affinity with writing for the stage. And in *Alice's Adventures in Wonderland* readers may be momentarily taken aback to find themselves repeatedly addressed by the author, who talks to them directly, as though conducting a conversation, and toys with their expectations. However, perhaps the most unusual feature is Dodgson's inclusion of literary short forms such as verses and songs, riddles and mental gymnastics, even a 'comic strip' for Father William, which not only put a strain on the overall coherence of the narrative as a literary form, but also – particularly when they are read aloud in different voices – invite a distinctly performative reading. In addition to this, an important part is also played by the typographic design of the text. Thus in *Through the Looking-Glass* there are blocks of asterisks plotting the movements of the literary figures on an imaginary chessboard. In Chapter 1, lines from a book that Alice finds in the Looking-Glass House are printed, logically enough, in mirror writing, and in Chapter 3 the 'extremely small voice' of an insect is represented by a smaller typeface.[10] There is also, of course, the famous mouse's tail that ends the mouse's tale in Chapter 3 of *Alice's Adventures in Wonderland* (p. 69).

The Embrace of *Alice* in the Nineteenth Century

In the wake of the success of the books, by the end of the nineteenth century there was already an *Alice* fashion, which has since turned into a full-scale *Alice* industry. What is par for the course nowadays must have been a considerable novelty in late-Victorian England, with the books being promoted on even the most banal of everyday objects.[11] Dodgson himself suggested a stamp case with illustrations by Tenniel, and he approved a biscuit tin with illustrations of *Through the Looking-Glass* produced by Manners. The board games and card games, dolls and figurines, and slides for magic lantern shows are of particular interest in that they more or less fleshed out the literary characters (p. 76). Away from the original narrative they could develop a life of their own. In games they

9. Unfortunately the design of many new editions and translations means that subtleties of this kind are not retained.

10. This is another effect that is not replicated in many new editions.

11. All such marketing strategies of course required Dodgson's explicit consent.

could enter into very different relationships to those in the books; figures could meet who were normally separated by chapter divisions. This familiarity through play significantly contributed to the Lewis Carroll characters taking root in the collective consciousness as symbolic figures. But it was not only in the realms of popular culture and the applied arts, it was also in the classical artistic disciplines that the *Alice* books were received with such intensity. They even had an impact in contemporary literature, with other writers appropriating the subject matter and imitating, adapting, poking fun at and plagiarising it in sequels, simulations and spin-offs.[12] Dodgson was flattered, rather than irritated, by his fellow-writers borrowing his literary creation, and on 11 September 1891 he noted in his diary that he had acquired some items for his own collection of *Alice* imitations. In addition to the diaries, a valuable record of Dodgson's self-image as a writer, and his awareness of the cultural context of his own time, has been preserved in his scrapbook of newspaper cuttings, into which he pasted articles or news reports, some of them relating to himself and his work, as well as texts he had published in various journals over the years.[13]

Inspired by the songs and poems in the *Alice* books, composers also soon turned their attention to Dodgson's creation. In 1870 William Boyd published a score entitled *The Songs from Alice's Adventures in Wonderland*, soon to be followed by *The Songs from Through the Looking-Glass* (1872). 1872 also saw the publication of Charles H.R. Marriott's *The Wonderland Quadrille* and *The Looking-Glass Quadrille*. Boyd's compositions were used in the first public presentation of *Alice in Wonderland*, put on by George Buckland at the Royal Polytechnic in London in summer 1876. It was billed as the 'new fanciful, spectacular, and musical entertainment, entitled Alice's Adventures; or The Queen of Hearts and the Missing Tarts' and was a mixture of acting and dramatic readings with musical interludes with Buckland in the role of narrator. Although this was the longest-running stage adaptation in London during Dodgson's lifetime, it did not meet his expectations of a full dramatisation and staging of the original work.[14] The second large-scale stage adaptation was Henry Savile Clarke's operetta *Alice in Wonderland, a Dream Play for Children*, in two acts, with music by Walter Slaughter, first performed on 23 December 1886 at the Prince of Wales Theatre in London (p. 78). This staging also combined dance, singing and acting. It was further note-worthy in that it combined both books in a single play, with one act devoted to each.

With the advent of film as a new medium of entertainment that was to take over from theatre, it was not long before the first moving-image version of *Alice* appeared, taking advantage of the technical possibilities of film to create images that could not be presented on stage, however sophisticated the production. On 17 October 1903 Cecil Hepworth and Percy Stow's *Alice in Wonderland* was premiered in the cinema. At 800 feet in length, the movie was the longest yet produced in Great Britain and ran for around twelve minutes. In 1910 the Edison Manufacturing Company presented the first American movie version, directed by Edwin S. Porter, and in 1915 W.W. Young created the first full-length movie with a running time of 52 minutes. Before Walt Disney released what was to become perhaps the best known adaptation, an animated cartoon, in 1951, he had already produced over fifty short so-called *Alice Comedies* in the 1920s, with the young Virginia Davis trying to find her way in a graphic Wonderland.

12. For more on parodies of *Alice*, see Carolyn Sigler's study and anthology, *Alternative Alices: Visions and Revisions of Lewis Carroll's Alice Books*, Lexington, KY: The University Press of Kentucky, 1997, and Peter Heath, 'Alician Parodies: A Checklist of Parodies of Alice', in *Jabberwocky*, vol. 13, no. 3, pp. 68–84.

13. Alice Liddell also retained a record of her own career as a literary figure. It was only in 2001 that her private archive of photographs taken of her by Dodgson, along with letters and documents, illustrated editions and toys, was auctioned. Alice Liddell is also probably the only real-life inspiration for a fictional character to have received an honorary doctorate. The title was conferred on her in 1932 by Columbia University, New York.

14. Dodgson toyed repeatedly with the notion of preparing *Alice* for the stage himself, but never carried it through, despite his great interest in the theatre and his numerous friendly contacts with that world. Over three hundred and eighty visits by him to the theatre have been verified on the basis of his diaries. As a young man he had already written plays for puppet theatre, a passion that he cultivated enthusiastically within his family circle; in 1856 he even presented a theatrical 'one-man show' including a magic lantern. On the stage history of *Alice* see Charles C. Lovett, *Alice on Stage: A History of the Early Theatrical Adaptions of 'Alice in Wonderland'*, Westport, CT and London: Meckler, 1989.

The Impact of *Alice* on the Visual Arts

Long before he became famous as a writer, Dodgson was already in close contact with the art world of his time. He was not only an enthusiastic and regular member of the audience in the theatre and at the opera, he also attended art exhibitions and made notes in his diary on what he had seen. In his diary entry of 13 June 1857 he records his first meeting with members of the Pre-Raphaelite Brotherhood who had come to Oxford to create the wall paintings in the new Debating Hall at the Oxford Union.[15] A photograph taken posthumously of his rooms at Christ Church shows, a little indistinctly, some of the paintings that he liked to have around him.[16] Dodgson also photographed many of his artist friends, notably Dante Gabriel Rossetti, with whose family he was in particularly close contact, but also William Holman Hunt, Arthur Hughes, Alexander Munro and John Everett Millais (p. 45).[17] There is a striking similarity, to name but one example, between Millais' portrait of his daughter Mary, entitled *Waking* 1865, and Dodgson's portrait of Alice, which tellingly bears the same title (p.48). In both portraits, the dominant characteristic is that of innocence – the innocence which so often underpins both Dodgson's portraits of children and the works of the Pre-Raphaelite artists, and which seems strangely other-worldly from our own perspective today.[18]

The first art movement that seriously engaged with *Alice* in the twentieth century, however, was Surrealism. In particular, Surrealist representations of dreams, which are constrained by neither the laws of nature nor the limitations of human reasoning, manifest parallels to the situations Alice experiences in her dream-travels in Wonderland and in the realms behind the looking-glass. Time and space seem to intermingle and categories such as duration and distance become strangely unreliable. In Dodgson's work, as in many Surrealist works, the alienation and misuse of everyday objects and poetic encounters with things that seem to make no sense become important artistic strategies that destabilise and cast doubt on the objectivity and conventions of 'reality'. Many Surrealists were drawn to the *Alice* books, not exclusively but principally because of the fascination they shared with Dodgson for the uncanny behind outward appearances and the unexpected that suddenly looms out of normality. In their eyes Dodgson was a Surrealist *avant la lettre*, an artistic predecessor and soulmate, whose literary worlds and characters seemed to prefigure many of their own anti-rationalist perspectives. That Surrealist allusions to *Alice* arise and can be identified on so many different levels merely underlines the complexity and multi-faceted nature of these references. Whereas some artists allude in their titles to the literary sources of their work, thus overtly prescribing a particular reading – witness René Magritte's various versions of *Alice au Pays des Merveilles* 1945–46 – other artists seem to have absorbed and internalised Dodgson's fantasy worlds to such an extent that the literary source is barely distinguishable from their own artistic innovation. The British Surrealists in particular have been described as the 'Children of Alice', highlighting their great indebtedness to the Victorian writer.[19]

In the context of the Surrealists' theoretical self-reflections, there are also numerous links to Dodgson. André Breton and Paul Eluard, for instance, included Dodgson's nonsense poem *The Hunting of the Snark* in their *Dictionnaire abrégée du Surréalisme* in 1938; just one year later, the 'Lobster Quadrille' from *Alice's Adventures in Wonderland* appeared in Breton's

15. He also made the acquaintance of John Ruskin (fig.), the prominent art critic and champion of the Pre-Raphaelites; the writers Alfred Tennyson and William Makepeace Thackeray; and the photographer Julia Margaret Cameron.

16. These included Arthur Hughes' *The Lady with the Lilacs* 1863, Sophie Anderson's *Minnie Morton* 1864 and *Girl with Lilacs* 1865, *Dreaming of Fairy Land* and *St. Cecilia* (both 1869) by Thomas Heaphy, and Alice Emily Donkin's *Waiting to Skate* c. 1874, based on one of Dodgson's photographs of Alexandra Kitchin. The reconstruction of Dodgson's collection is to the credit of Edward Wakeling, the editor of Dodgson's diaries, and I gratefully acknowledge his generous suggestions and pointers.

17. Ultimately it was also thanks to promptings from his artistic friends (the writers Henry Kingsley and George MacDonald, who encouraged Dodgson to consider publishing his manuscript) that *Alice's Adventures in Wonderland* found its way to Alexander Macmillan of the London publishing house Macmillan and Company.

18. It is fair to assume that this idealisation of childhood, which – as in the photographs of Julia Margaret Cameron, for instance – even included the stylised portrayal of children as angels, was not least influenced by the high rate of infant mortality at that time.

19. By 1936 Dodgson's own drawings were already being included in the exhibition *Fantastic Art, Dada, Surrealism* at the Museum of Modern Art, New York.

Max Ernst
The Stolen Mirror, 1941

20. On the Surrealists' reception of *Alice*, see Rüdiger von Tiedemann, 'Alice bei den Surrealisten. Zur Rezeption Lewis Carrolls', in *Internationale Zeitschrift für Literaturwissenschaft*, vol. 17, parts 1–3, 1982, pp. 61–80.

21. Max Ernst was also a key figure for many artists in the 1960s and 1970s, particularly for Robert Smithson, whose interest in the *Alice* books will be discussed later.

22. The experience of war as a historical context is also central to Oskar Kokoschka's painting *Anschluss [Annexation] – Alice in Wonderland* of 1941 (ill.); similarly, there is an implicit political connection in Magritte's *Alice* paintings. The grinning pear is a reference to a caricature by Honoré Daumier, depicting Louis Philippe, 'King of the French'. It is interesting to note in this context that political cartoons in the 1930s and 1940s often deployed figures from the Alice books. In 1939 James Dyrenforth and Max Kester satirised National Socialist Germany in *Adolf in Blunderland*.

23. The portraits of *Alice* and *Napoleon in the Wilderness* were hung together in Ernst's 1942 exhibition at the Valentine Gallery in New York. For more on this, see Sarah Wilson, 'Die Begegnung mit Albion und Alice – Max Ernst in England', in Werner Spies (ed.), *Max Ernst – Retrospektive zum 100. Geburtstag*, Munich: Prestel, 1991, pp. 363–73.

Anthologie de l'humour noir, and in 1941 Eluard included excerpts from *The Hunting of the Snark* and *Through the Looking-Glass* in his book *Poésie involontaire et poésie intentionelle*.[20] There are clear parallels between Dodgson's literary strategies and the poetics of the Surrealists, with regard to the focus and artistic exploration of the recognition and attribution of meaning as a cognitive process based on sensory perceptions.

Besides dreams, mirrors as both symbols and metaphors are a central motif in the Surrealists' responses to *Alice*. However, far from reflecting an image of the world laid out before them, they project a Surrealist take on reality and expose the things that we otherwise do not see. In that light, Balthus' *Alice dans le miroir* 1933 has to be read as an unreliable mirror. The very title is ambiguous with regard to the status of the picture itself. Is it an image of Alice contemplating herself in the mirror or does it portray Alice gazing out of the realm behind the looking-glass? Is it a painted reflection or is the picture itself to be read as a mirror? Which in turn raises the question as to why it does not reflect us, the viewers – and why Alice, whose form does appear in the tricky mirror image, is not standing next to us. For that matter, is the young woman even the Alice that we know from the books?

By the same token, Max Ernst's painting *The Stolen Mirror* 1941 poses more questions regarding its status and function as a mirror than it gives pointers to a conclusive interpretation (p. 15). Ernst engaged more than any other Surrealist with the work of Dodgson. Between 1939 and 1970 he produced numerous works that directly alluded to *Alice* or that can be seen to relate to that world.[21] In 1939, when Ernst was in southern France, interned as a German-born enemy alien, he painted *Alice in 1939* (p. 110). As a prisoner of war at Les Milles he experimented with the technique of decalcomania in his paintings. Two years later, following a series of escapes, releases, recaptures and re-imprisonments in France, then annexed by the Nazi regime, Ernst finally escaped to the United States where he painted the sequel, entitled *Alice in 1941* (p. 111). This painting and *The Stolen Mirror* would appear to be the first compositions Ernst made following his arrival in the USA. However, since it is known that he had some decalcomanias with him during his dramatic escape from France to Spain, his point of departure for the United States, it may also be that he produced these works while he was still on the run. Whatever the case, they clearly relate closely to Ernst's experience of war, displacement, escape and hope of protection in a distant land.[22] In 1944, at the exhibition *The Imagery of Chess* at the Julien Levy Gallery in New York, Ernst showed not only a chess game but also the sculpture *The King Playing with the Queen* (p. 115). In 1957 he painted *Pour les amis d'Alice* and in 1964 *Alice envoie des messages aux poissons*. Concurrent with these paintings, from 1950 onwards he also produced a number of illustrated books such as *La Chasse au snark* (1950), *Logique sans peine* (1966), *The Hunting of the Snark* (1968) and *Lewis Carroll's Wunderhorn* (1970).

The expansion of literary allusions and the encryption of the literary reference which so many artists – not just Surrealists – actively engage in is perfectly exemplified in the work of Max Ernst. The fictive portraits *Alice in 1939* and *Alice in 1941* depict the figure of a woman, surrounded by reddish-orange decalcomanic growths. This female figure is distinctly reminiscent of those in other paintings of this period, such as the different versions of *The Antipope* 1940/41, 1942 and *Napoleon in the Wilderness* 1941.[23] This similarity alone can of course not be taken as evidence that these are all depictions of the same woman or that they all derive from the same source, namely *Alice's Adventures in Wonderland*. It may well be that Leonora Carrington, who was living with Ernst at the time, played an important part *as* Alice. A sense of this process of artistic encryption may be derived from a poem by Ernst, which he published in 1958 in the catalogue for an exhibition at the Galerie Creuzevault in Paris:

> Présence d'Alice
>
> At the junction of two signs, one for a school of herrings and the other for a school of crystals, thirty-three little girls set out for the white butterfly hunt, the blind dance in the night, princes sleep badly and the black crow is to speak.

Six phrases from this poem also serve as the titles of paintings by Ernst between 1957 and 1958; although they do not overtly refer to the *Alice* books, the allusion in the title of the poem shifts them into the misty terrain of Ernst's reception of *Alice* (p. 112). Rather than the title providing a definite reference, it is more of a fluid allusion and a latently productive generator of associations.

A similarly diffuse Alice figure may also be observed in the work of Salvador Dalí. In 1969 he produced a series of prints, each including a girl with a skipping rope, who was to be explicitly identified in a sculpture from 1977 entitled *Alice in Wonderland* (p. 116). Yet the same girl, swinging a skipping rope, also appears in his early work, without any direct reference to Alice;[24] the later, retrospective explicit naming of the girl as *the* Alice necessitates a re-reading of Dalí's early work. As in the work of Max Ernst, the Alice references in Dalí's œuvre prove to be a complex yet playful artistic strategy that both specifies and opens up references to the literary source.[25]

Unearthing *Alice*

To this day there can be a productive friction between allusions intended by artists, in so far as they are not made explicit, and the associations in the viewer's mind. In addition to works that openly refer to *Alice*, such as Duane Michal's *Alice's Mirror* 1974 (p. 140) or Marcel Broodthaers' *Cartes d'Alice in Wonderland* 1972, there are works from the 1960s and 1970s – exploring linguistic codes and conventions, the reliability of text and images as means of representation, and the resilience of signs in general – that invite readings against a backdrop of the same issues relating to physiological perception, epistemology and linguistic confusions that Alice constantly has to contend with.

The seemingly clear, transparent works produced in the context of Minimalism and Conceptual art have a particular focus on perception and the foundations of cognition. Systematic and logical approaches, mathematically calculating progressions or permutations and their schematic, almost scientific representations emphasise the logical rather than the individual or original expression.[26] They deliberately *under*challenge the artistically conditioned eye, by focusing on the seemingly obvious. Although they may appear to be self-explanatory and tautological, such works reflect the path to cognition as a process and raise questions, concerning the relativity of cognition and the objectivisability of the seemingly obvious, the power of interpretation and

24. This group of works includes the two paintings entitled *Morphological Echo* 1934–36, as well as the painting *Nostalgic Echo* 1935, the monumental *Landscape with Girl Skipping Rope* 1936, and the two small-format works *Average Pagan Landscape* and *Anthropomorphic Echo* (both 1937). In 1936 Dalí integrated his own *Nostalgic Echo* into the painting *Suburbs of the Paranoiac-critical City: Afternoon on the Outskirts of European History*. The same girl also appears in the Surrealist animated cartoon *Destino*, made by Dalí in collaboration with Walt Disney, which was begun in 1946 but not finished until 2003. Later she appears as Daphne in the prints *Daphne I* and *Daphne II*.

25. The motif of a girl with a skipping rope in Dalí's work derives from a religious tradition, that is to say, a specifically anthropomorphic church bell in the form of a female figure with a wide skirt.

26. As a mathematician, Charles Dodgson had a strong fascination with logic for many years which culminated in two publications for a general readership in 1886 and 1896.

authority, control and impotence, hierarchy and autonomy, which ultimately connect aesthetic contemplation with aspects of identity construction and with political issues. This, too, may call to mind Alice's disputes with the supposed power-brokers in Wonderland and in the realms through the looking-glass. Dodgson's narratives continually return to issues such as how we understand what we see, what proof actually proves and how very much our perspective is determined by our position. And above all, from the point of the view of the child, they also delve into who is talking and who is listening.[27]

Take artists such as Joseph Kosuth or Robert Smithson. Bearing in mind the importance of experiencing time as it is expressed in different chapters of the *Alice* books, a work such as *Clock (One and Five)* 1965/1997 (p. 126) dealing with the representation, the nature and construction of time can quite easily be related to *Alice*.[28] Although little could be proved only from gazing at the work, one might nevertheless argue that Kosuth has engaged with Dodgson in other works, and not only with his literary output, but also – as in *Function* 1970 – with his mathematical and logical work.[29] In the case of Robert Smithson, although none of his art works appears to refer explicitly to *Alice*, he does refer more than once to the Alice books in his theoretical writing.[30] In the early text *Iconography of Desolation* (c. 1962) Smithson quotes the episode of the Pool of Tears to express substantial doubts about the objectivity of artistic representation and to enlarge on the healing quality of ancient art forms. In the work *Untitled (Tear)* 1961-63 that seems to relate to this text one finds tears as written words dripping down eyes, creating a kind of flood of despair at the bottom of the work (p. 144). At the same time a drawing such as *A Heap of Language* 1966 emphasises the plasticity, one could also say the gravity, of written language as the words pile up like bricks to build a sculptural form.[31] Smithson's use of maps, folding them or cutting them apart to rearrange them, plays not only with graphic representations of space but also with our sense of orientation. And, most importantly, in many of his works mirrors reflect the world surrounding the work within the work, breaking down the border between the space of symbolic representation and what is considered our shared reality; or they seem to reflect, project and virtually complete sculptural arrangements. It may have been Smithson's fascination with such effects and phenomena of perception that triggered his interest in *Alice*; equally, it could well be that this fascination arose from his reading of Dodgson's books.

As Conceptual art dropped the brush and took hold of the word, the written inscription became a significant instrument of artistic expression, focusing on the material presence of language and its inconsistencies as a source of meaning – and provoking questions concerning the understanding of both what art is intended to be and the system that legitimises it. It is in this context of what is now often referred to as a *linguistic turn* that the text made its way into the domain of the 'white cube' and the museum as institutions of the visual arts. It was this intellectual movement that brought visual art close to the field of literature and philosophy.

Iconography and the Interpretation of the *Alice* Books

One of the most remarkable facts concerning the history of *Alice's Adventures in Wonderland* is that it has been so consistently reissued and republished that

27. Last but not least, the medium of language not only to convey artistic concepts but also in the sense of the realisation of an idea, as well as the notion of the book as an artistic frame and medium of distribution, has become an important means of artistic expression in the visual arts. The purposeful and conceptual artistic use of the specific structure of the book that Carroll practises in the *Alice* books can be observed in many contemporary artists' books.

28. Of course, it is not only Dodgson who has influenced Kosuth but also the whole tradition of logic and analytical philosophy, from Plato to Charles Sanders Peirce, Ferdinand de Saussure and Ludwig Wittgenstein. However, it surely is no surprise that it was in the 1960s that the connection between Carroll and Wittgenstein, for example, began to be explored.

29. In the print *Map to Indicate (E.L., L.C.)* 1992 Kosuth quotes a line from Carroll's novel *Sylvie and Bruno*.

30. Other texts with references to *Alice* are *Entropy and the New Monuments* (1966) and *A Museum of Language in the Vicinity of Art* (1968). Smithson also had a long-playing record with a reading of *Alice's Adventures in Wonderland*. An edition of the book with his own annotations has survived in the artist's library, documenting his particular interests in different passages.

31. In contrast, Marcel Broodthaers in *Rebus* 1973 focuses more on a cryptographic encoding of the written word.

it has never been out of print. An important moment in the history of the editions and reception of *Alice* came in 1907, when the copyright for *Alice's Adventures in Wonderland* expired and countless illustrators set to work, devising their own versions. By late autumn of that year there were already at least fourteen new illustrated editions on sale, in time for the Christmas market. Bearing in mind the importance of the pictoriality of the work as a whole, these new editions could in fact be described as new interpretations.[32] And in all probability this is precisely what makes this work such a stimulating and productive challenge for illustrators. This constant updating of *Alice* with new illustrations and illustrated editions has meant that the characters and settings of the two books – Alice and other figures such as the Hatter, the White Rabbit, the Caterpillar on the mushroom and many more – have become highly recognisable icons in their own right.

In particular, it is Alice's characteristic clothing – the blue dress and the white pinafore – that lets us recognise her easily even today, a code whose sources go back to the nineteenth century. Both *The Nursery 'Alice'* and the biscuit tin produced by Manners with illustrations from *Through the Looking-Glass* used blue and white in Alice's clothes; and the combination was canonised in the Little Folks Edition of 1903, with coloured illustrations featuring Alice in blue dress and white pinafore, the costume by which she would forever after be identified. Thus the girl in Balthus' painting *The Street*, wearing a blue and white dress, can be read as an allusion to Alice, even if the scene itself is pure invention (p. 20).[33] Similarly freely invented scenes make up Anna Gaskell's *Wonder* 1996, a series of photographs that narrates a story with Alice as the main figure, which is very different to the original (p. 152). The considerable extent of the series might even seem to suggest that these are illustrations for some other, lost text or version of *Alice*. At the same time, the components of this series appear to make up an independent picture-story that has no need of the written word. Once again, the Alice figures are recognisable as such by virtue of their clothing.

Other artists, such as for instance Sigmar Polke, refer to *Alice* by citing Tenniel's illustrations (p. 130). However, the allusion is not confined to the gesture of citation alone, or in a reference to some literary source. The choice of a particular pictorial quotation is a significant artistic decision, which sees the image being extracted from its original *con-text*, placed in a new situation and hence imbued with new meaning. Artists who overtly cite the visual imagery of Dodgson's books establish a relationship between their works and his texts, triggering associations, appealing to viewers' powers of recollection and inviting them to *read* the work through the lens of the literary source.[34] In 1971, when Polke adopted the Caterpillar from Chapter 5 of *Alice's Adventures in Wonderland*, it was not by chance that he chose a figure that was synonymous in the 1960s and 1970s with drugs and altered states of mind, thus making the connection with the same psychedelic culture that features in Adrian Piper's hallucinatory triptych *Alice in Wonderland* 1966 (p. 134).[35] Less interested in the mind-bending and sense-expanding effects of marihuana, LSD and mushrooms, when Marshall McLuhan and Quentin Fiore considered the same illustration in their artists' book, *The Medium is the Message*, it was with reference to a question, the question 'Who are *you*?' which the Caterpillar addresses to Alice – the question of the constitution and construction of identity in a society saturated by the influence of mass media.

32. In that sense, translations into other languages, hampered by the untranslatability of certain wordplays, also have to be regarded as reinterpretations.

33. Significantly, this painting was made in 1933, the same year as his *Alice dans le miroir*.

34. The topic of memory is of course one of the central subjects in the *Alice* books in connection to the construction of identity.

35. Adrian Piper's triptych was also part of the exhibition *Summer of Love* at Tate Liverpool in 2005, and the illustration of the caterpillar scene by Mervyn Peake featured in the exhibition *High Society* at the Wellcome Collection in London in 2010.

Balthus
The Street, 1933

Mary Heilman
Go Ask Alice, 2006

In the œuvre of Kiki Smith, the works with a connection to Alice may be seen in the wider context of her interest not only in young girls as literary figures, but also in friendships between animals and people, above all as they feature in fairytales. In this light, the moment in the narrative when Alice is in danger of drowning in her own tears must have had a particular appeal for Smith. In her series of prints on this subject, she engages with the three illustrations from that chapter in the manuscript and appropriates them by drawing in the style of Dodgson himself. These large-format aquatint etchings, *Pool of Tears 1*, *Pool of Tears 2 (after Lewis Carroll)* and *Come Away from Her After Lewis Carroll* 2000, are enlarged versions – one might almost describe them as *retellings* – of Dodgson's original drawings in the order in which they appear in the manuscript (p. 160).

The potential complexity of the interplay of *Alice* reception and references, the extent to which various *Alice* allusions may refer not only to the literary source but also to each other, is exemplified in Mary Heilman's painting *Go Ask Alice* 2006 (p. 21). The bright pattern of differently coloured squares, apparently receding into the distance like a perspectival landscape, alludes to the illustration of the countryside, marked out like a chess board, in Chapter 2 of *Through the Looking-Glass*. Meanwhile the title of the painting cites the title of a book, published anonymously in 1971, which in turn – it has been suggested – took its title from the track 'White Rabbit' on the 1967 album *Surrealistic Pillow* by Jefferson Airplane, which was very much part of the psychedelic subculture of that time. The book itself is about a teenage girl addicted to drugs, who, in a variation on Alice in her own wonderland, tries to find her own path.

The Sensuality of the Written

When contemporary artists such as Fiona Banner, Rodney Graham, Gary Hill or Tim Rollins engage not only with themes from the *Alice* books, but also with the materiality of literary communication, there has to be a close connection with their original interest in this literary source.[36] You might say that they unhinge the text from the book: they take the book apart and make it their own, superimposing other works on it, they *translate* it and *cite* it. They investigate ways in which the content of a narrative can be communicated using visual art. They focus on the visual qualities of the written word, the aesthetic form of the book and the sensuality of the act of reading.[37] And these productive readings appear to be inspired not only by the books' philosophical content, but also by the unusual structure of their literary form and the meaning of the materiality of the *Alice* books.

In the video *Why Do Things Get in a Muddle (Come on Petunia)* 1984 Gary Hill staged a fictive conversation between a girl – wearing the readily recognisable blue dress and white pinafore – and her father.[38] On closer examination, not only is the girl's clothing reminiscent of that of Alice, the camera also constantly plays with effects arising from perspectival distortion and movement that could well call to mind the growing and shrinking figure of Alice on her adventures. Closer listening to the spoken text reveals that the soundtrack is a combination of quotations from *Through the Looking-Glass* and excerpts from Gregory Bateson's *Steps to an Ecology of Mind* (1971). The performance of passages taken from these works presented in the form of a conversation – the

36. Whereas other artists choose to quote the iconography of the *Alice* books, these artists, one might say, choose to work with the written word, referring to the textual nature of their source.

37. Like their literary source, many of the works these artists have produced are text-image compounds that interweave reading with seeing – at least to the degree that the aesthetic, visual qualities of the text play an important role.

38. The subtitle of this work is in fact an anagram of the well known phrase 'Once upon a time' which begins so many fairy-tales.

cited passages essentially focus on how language constitutes meaning – blends the sources and makes them difficult to distinguish. But the viewer must also listen closely for another reason: during the shooting of the video, large sections of the texts were spoken backwards by the two actors and only turned back round – or mirrored – during the editing process (p. 164).

Tim Rollins created a collective reading of *Alice's Adventures in Wonderland*, made in 1989 under the auspices of his social art project and collective Kids of Street. He and the members of KOS literally took apart a copy of the book and pasted the pages onto a large-format canvas so that the whole book was visible at a glance. During the process, as the participants engaged with the text, they selected the illustration, from the original manuscript, of Alice squeezed into the White Rabbit's house to replicate on the picture ground of book pages. This enlarged image vanishes behind a monochrome colour plane. In the same year, Rodney Graham placed an old copy of *Alice's Adventures in Wonderland* in a casket which, for its part, cites a sculpture by Donald Judd. Here, too, the text becomes invisible, withdrawn from the reader's reach, by being concealed in a protective sculptural container. For *Arsewoman in Wonderland Act I* 2001 Fiona Banner transcribed the action of the erotic movie *Asswoman in Wonderland* (1998). In a highly ironic manner Banner translates the sexually transgressive parody, which is primarily about visual sexual stimulation, back into a written text. The text is printed in bright pink writing on a large-format poster with a second poster installed next to it on which the same text is mirrored upside down and right to left. Together, these two panels look almost like the spread of a book. Although this presentation of the text is scarcely conducive to reading it through, nevertheless the viewer's eye is repeatedly caught by precisely those words and formulations that recall the vocabulary of the original literary source (p. 156). Here, too, we witness the complex multi-layered reference that characterises allusions to *Alice* in the contemporary arts.

In Conclusion

Drawn from many different sources, a literary work of art is made of multiple writings, entering into mutual relations of dialogue, parody and contestation. And the place where this multiplicity is focused is not the author, but in fact the reader.[39] References by visual artists to *Alice* operate across a spectrum that ranges from overt, explicit connections to complex allusions which, like the Cheshire Cat, tend to vanish from sight, or at least are far from immediately apparent. And on that basis – entirely logically and only slightly tongue-in-cheek – it can be said that in the visual arts equally, a reference to *Alice* can always be legitimately claimed whenever we, as the viewer, be it museum visitor, art critic or exhibition curator, discern one and declare it to be so. And of course there are also occasions when the viewer makes a connection that was never intended – spotting a grin, one's mind naturally turns to *the* cat. Indeed, even in the case of an outright misunderstanding, a *mis*interpretation would appear to be both legitimate and productive – a fruitful echo of the polysemy of Dodgson's works, in which meaning is never a simple matter, but a rich field of contestation, multiplicity and play.

39. This change of perspective was expressed by the French philosopher Roland Barthes in his text 'The Death of the Author' (1969), as well as by Michel Foucault in his essay 'What is an Author?' (1969).

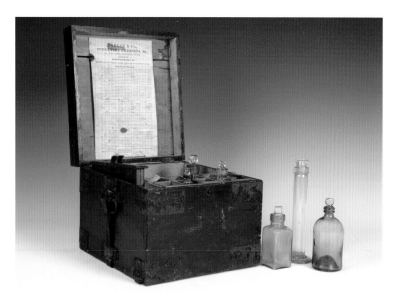

top: Charles L. Dodgson's Wet-Collodion Photographic Outfit, c.1860

bottom: Ottewill Folding Box Camera, 1853

above: Oscar Gustav Rejlander
Lewis Carroll (Rev. Charles L. Dodgson), 28 March 1863

right: Unknown artist
Charles L. Dodgson 1852–1860

Charles L. Dodgson
The Dream, August 1863

Charles L. Dodgson
St. George and the Dragon, 26 June 1875

top: Charles L. Dodgson
Alice Pleasance Liddell, Spring 1860

bottom: Charles L. Dodgson
Alice Pleasance Liddell; Lorina Charlotte
('Ina') Liddell; Edith Mary Liddell, July 1860

far right: Charles L. Dodgson
Alice Pleasance Liddell, Summer 1858

Charles L. Dodgson
Lorina Charlotte Liddell; Alice Pleasance Liddell;
Edith Mary Liddell, 1858–1860

Charles L. Dodgson
Edith Mary Liddell; Lorina Charlotte ('Ina') Liddell;
Alice Pleasance Liddell, Summer 1858

Julia Margaret Cameron
Alice Pleasance Liddell as 'Alethea', September 1872

right: Alexander Bassano
Alice, Edith and Ina Liddell, c.1876

Charles L. Dodgson
Watercolour of the Liddell children, 1862

right: Sir William Blake Richmond
The Sisters, 1864

Edward Wakeling

Lewis Carroll

– and the –

Victorian Art World

Charles L. Dodgson
William Holman Hunt, 30 June 1860

From an early age Charles L. Dodgson (1832–98), better known as Lewis Carroll, was interested in art. His large Victorian middle-class family had access to paintings and sculpture through publications such as *The Art Journal*, and they created hand-written magazines that circulated within the family, with Charles as the main organiser and contributor. From the age of around 13, Dodgson began a series of domestic magazines that contained stories and poems, serialised adventures, drawings, and reviews of books and art. In *The Rectory Umbrella*, the seventh of the magazines, composed between 1850 and 1853, Dodgson parodied paintings in the Vernon Gallery, his own juvenile draughtsmanship showing skill and humour.[1] He enjoyed sketching, both comic and serious subjects, but was never entirely satisfied with his own artistic achievements. With the introduction of the new black art of photography, he found a source of aesthetic endeavour that he could excel in.

Dodgson was a mathematician by profession and university lecturer at Christ Church, Oxford. He became a pioneer photographer in 1856, adopting the wet collodion process within five years of its invention. At this time, photographers fell into two camps: commercial practitioners and amateur artists. Dodgson belonged to the latter group. His œuvre of almost 3000 photographs spans 25 years, portraiture being his main focus. He had a particular skill in photographing children despite long exposure times and the fidgety nature of young people, entrancing them with wonderful stories so that the moment of calm he required to obtain a sharp image seemed effortless and natural. Some surviving accounts by children of being photographed by Dodgson record the joy and excitement of the moment when they sat before his camera, rather than the tedium and stillness enforced by other photographers. He was interested in

composition and arrangement, and he learnt much from the artists of his day. For example, his knowledge of paintings helped him to group his sitters and arrange their hands so that they looked natural and pleasing to the eye. Particularly in his later photography, Dodgson explicitly followed the tradition of Victorian tableaux, with children dressed in costumes representing a literary event or idea. Dodgson collected and borrowed dressing-up material for this purpose – theatrical costumes, oriental and exotic costumes from around the world, and fancy-dress, often made by the mothers of the children.

Based at Oxford, Dodgson was easily able to get to London by railway, and these excursions invariably meant a visit to an art gallery and exhibition. His surviving diaries reveal that he often spent many hours at the Royal Academy during its summer exhibitions, viewing the latest work of living artists.[2] For example, in 1855 he 'paid a long visit to the RA' on 21 June, and later 'went to the Gallery of the British Artists where I scarcely got the worth of my shilling'.[3] He had the ability to discriminate between what he saw as good and inferior work, preferring the paintings of the Pre-Raphaelite Movement and a select few of the other artists of his day, guided by the critical eye of John Ruskin. Dodgson read Ruskin's published works avidly, and the two men met in Christ Church Common Room on 27 October 1857, Dodgson noting: 'I had a little conversation with him, but not enough to bring out anything characteristic or striking in him. His appearance was rather disappointing, a general feebleness of expression, with no commanding air, or any external signs of deep thought, as one would have expected to see in such a man.'[4] Nevertheless, they became lifelong friends, and met and corresponded in friendly terms, Dodgson relying on Ruskin's artistic wisdom and advice. Clearly, Dodgson admired the

1. Robert Vernon's gift to the nation of 152 pictures by British artists was made to the National Gallery in 1847, and parts of the collection were engraved and published in book form in 1850.

2. Dodgson maintained a diary throughout his life, recording significant events rather than making a report each day. The early years are missing, as too are four key years from 1858 to 1862, but the remaining nine volumes, spanning 1855 to 1898, are now housed in the British Library. They were published for the first time in an unabridged form by the Lewis Carroll Society, edited by Edward Wakeling (Luton and Clifford, 1993–2007).

3. Edward Wakeling (ed.), *Lewis Carroll's Diaries*, vol. 1, Luton, 1993, pp. 103–4.

4. Edward Wakeling (ed.), *Lewis Carroll's Diaries*, vol. 3, Luton, 1995, p. 122.

honesty of Pre-Raphaelite painting and, in time, became personally acquainted with the artists, visiting their homes and studios, and even taking photographic portraits of them.

Dodgson's acquaintance with the Pre-Raphaelites began in August 1857 when a group of Oxford University men elected to decorate the walls of the Oxford Union building with Arthurian paintings. The Oxford Union was established in 1823 as a forum for free discussion and debate. Dodgson's uncle Hassard Hume Dodgson was one of the Union's earliest supporters, becoming President in 1826. Dodgson was admitted to the Union in March 1857, although he had some reservations, noting 'it might be worth while *now* to be a member … I have avoided it hitherto, as it would have been too great a temptation to wasting time.'[5] The new debating hall, designed by Benjamin Woodward (he was photographed by Dodgson), was first used in February 1857. Six months later, the task of decorating the hall was begun. The main artists were Dante Gabriel Rossetti, whose idea it was, William Morris, and Edward Burne-Jones. Joining them were John Hungerford Pollen (of Merton College), Valentine Cameron Prinsep, John Roddam Spencer Stanhope (of Christ Church), Arthur Hughes, and William Rivière. The sculptor Alexander Munro also became part of this artistic group. Dodgson took an interest in the murals in the debating hall and admired the work of these new young artists, later photographing five of them, and commissioning one to paint for him.

An evening party in November 1857 at the home of Dr Henry Acland, Professor of Medicine at Oxford, resulted in Dodgson scrutinising some original drawings and photographs. Acland showed Dodgson a drawing by Ruskin of a skeleton hand, some sketches made by Dean Henry Liddell when he was an undergraduate, and a photograph of a sculpture by Munro entitled *Children's Play*. This latter photograph was much admired, and Acland offered to see whether he could get a copy for Dodgson. A few months later, this promise was honoured. On 22 February 1858, Mrs Acland invited Dodgson to meet Munro at her home, and suggested that Dodgson show some of his photographs. Dodgson wrote in his diary that Munro 'promised to send me a second picture of his group … and begged I would look in at his studio … when next in town. He suggests that I should photograph his bust of Dante, which Dr Acland has.'[6] Thus began a friendship that lasted the rest of Munro's short life.

Dodgson visited Munro's London studio with his brother, Edwin, in April 1858 and recorded: 'he showed us over his studio, containing, among many half-finished designs, four statues which are going to the Royal Academy tomorrow. He has a large collection of photographs, many from his own sculpture; one he gave me … He gave me carte-blanche to photograph anything and everything in his studio, when I come to town in June, whether he is there or not. It is a tempting inducement to take my camera there.'[7] Dodgson made the trip to Munro's studio and photographed several works – busts and statues of famous people, and sculptures of his patron's children. The Victorians much admired the child-figure in art, generally as a symbol of innocence. The high level of infant mortality made them conscious of the precarious nature of childhood, and many of the more wealthy parents took the opportunity to commission an artist to capture an image of their offspring. Munro already had a collection of photographs to record his work and was pleased to have Dodgson's assistance to record his more recent work. Photography was used by many Victorian painters, sculptors, and illustrators both as an aid in their work and as a means of recording their paintings.[8]

5. Ibid., p. 27.

6. Ibid., p. 157.

7. Ibid., pp. 173–74.

8. Some photographers, such as Oscar Rejlander and Henry Peach Robinson, initially trained as painters, and supplied anatomical and composition photographs to artists.

right: Charles L. Dodgson
Dante Gabriel Rossetti, 6 October 1863

below: Charles L. Dodgson
John Everett Millais, 21 July 1865

bottom right: Charles L. Dodgson
Alexander Munro and Wife, 7 October 1863

Dodgson's friendship with Munro opened the door to other significant artists of the day. On 21 July 1863, Munro took Dodgson to visit Arthur Hughes. Dodgson wrote in his diary: 'We went together to Wandsworth, and called on Mr A. Hughes, and saw some lovely pictures, and his four little children, one of whom is painted in *The Woodman's Return*. He also is to come, with his children to be photographed.'[9] Also known as *Home from Work*, this painting was exhibited at the Royal Academy in 1861. On a second visit a few days later, Dodgson noted: 'I arranged to take the little picture he is painting.'[10] The picture that Arthur Hughes was painting was called *The Lady with the Lilacs*, possibly a study for *Silver and Gold*. Almost three months later Dodgson noted on 7 October: 'Mr Hughes told me that the picture I bought of his is finished, and we arranged that he should bring it (as well as the children to be photographed) ... on Monday.'[11] The painting, a half-length study of a young woman with her right hand raised, as if to pick a lilac blossom, subsequently hung in Dodgson's sitting-room at Christ Church above the fireplace. He photographed the Hughes family on 12 October 1863.[12]

Alexander Munro was also instrumental in introducing Dodgson to Dante Gabriel Rossetti. Munro took Dodgson to Rossetti's Chelsea home on 30 September 1863, where Dodgson saw 'some very lovely pictures, most of them only half finished'.[13] Dodgson continued: 'He was most hospitable in his offers of the use of house and garden for picture-taking, and I arranged to take my camera there on Monday.' On the same day, Dodgson visited the studio of William Holman Hunt, and saw him at work on *The Afterglow in Egypt*. Dodgson began a

four-day photographic session at Rossetti's home on 6 October 1863, taking pictures of the Rossetti clan, friends who called, such as Charles Cayley (the classics translator) and Alphonse Legros (the French painter and sculptor), some of Rossetti's models, and a portfolio of Rossetti's drawings. Clearly, Dodgson was in his element, enjoying this foray into an artistic world not normally accessible to others. He was just beginning to make his name as an amateur photographer, but he was still unknown as the writer Lewis Carroll; the *Alice* books were yet to be published.[14]

By now, Dodgson was well acquainted with two founders of the Pre-Raphaelite Brotherhood, Rossetti and Holman Hunt, but he was keen to meet the third. He was familiar with the work of John Everett Millais, which he had seen exhibited. On 7 April 1864, armed with a letter of introduction from Holman Hunt, Dodgson set out to meet Millais in person. He recorded in his diary:

> I first went to 7A by mistake, and while waiting at the door noticed a gentleman who was walking up and down in front of the next house, and whom I thought like the pictures of Millais. We interchanged some remarks about the difficulty of getting the door answered. Then came some children with a governess, and I said to myself 'there comes *My First Sermon*,' but they passed the door I was at, made a rush at the gentleman (evidently their father), and went into the next

9. Edward Wakeling (ed.), *Lewis Carroll's Diaries*, vol. 4, Luton, 1997, pp. 223–24.

10. Ibid., p. 230.

11. Ibid., p. 254.

12. Prints of Dodgson's photographs were usually presented to the sitters and their parents, often inscribed 'From the Artist', confirming his status as a non-commercial photographer. However, if parents wanted additional copies, Dodgson made a nominal charge for these.

13. *Diaries*, vol. 4, p. 243. The unfinished paintings by Rossetti are not identified, but Dodgson photographed a series of drawings a few days later. In June 1864, Dodgson saw Rossetti working on *Venus Verticordia*, which, he noted, 'will be very beautiful; it represents Venus (head and shoulders), with some butterflies hovering round her head: the back-ground is to be roses' (ibid., p. 316).

14. *Alice's Adventures in Wonderland* was first published in November 1865.

house. At last I found out my mistake, and that the gentleman was Millais himself: he was very kind, and took me into his studio … and sent for his children – two boys, and three girls.[15]

This introduction led to a photographic session with the family in July 1865 during which Mr and Mrs Millais and two of their daughters were photographed. Mary Millais was photographed by Dodgson in a portrait he entitled *Waking*. In the same month Millais began a painting of his daughter which he also called *Waking*, but it is not clear who had the first inspiration.

Another artist whom Dodgson admired was Sophie Anderson. French by birth, she came to England in 1854, and exhibited frequently at the British Institution and the Royal Academy. Dodgson saw her picture *Rosy Morn* exhibited in April 1864 and he described it as the 'loveliest of all' the paintings in the exhibition; 'the head and arms of a child leaning with one elbow on a pillow, with dreamy, Sant-like eyes'.[16] On the same day that Dodgson paid his first short visit to the Millais family, he decided to make a call on the Andersons, Sophie and her husband, Walter, also a renowned artist. He noted: 'I found them at home, very pleasant people, but there were no pictures in the house except some half-coloured sketches of heads – all exceedingly pretty.'[17] In June 1864, Dodgson purchased one of Sophie Anderson's paintings; entitled *Minnie Morton*, it subsequently hung in his rooms at Christ Church. When his sister, Mary, married in April 1869, he gave her the picture as a wedding gift, but he asked Anderson to make a copy for him. He also photographed the picture, so it was clearly a painting he much admired. In 1865, he made another purchase from Sophie Anderson. He wrote on 6 July: 'Paid another visit to the Royal Academy, then to the Andersons, where I saw several beautiful pictures,

left: Charles L. Dodgson
John Ruskin, 3 June 1875

above: Charles L. Dodgson
Assisted self portrait at Croft Rectory, July/August 1857

15. *Diaries*, vol. 4, pp. 288–89.

16. Ibid., p. 285. His reference was to the artist James Sant, whom Dodgson later met in April 1866.

17. Ibid., p. 290.

and gave Mr Anderson some hints on the perspective of a picture of his, which will lead to his altering it a good deal. I bought a little picture by Mrs Anderson, of a child's head in profile: the original was in the house, and was called into the room, a beautiful child about 12, Elizabeth Turnbull by name. I intend taking a photograph of her in the same attitude as the picture.'[18] The picture was entitled *Girl with Lilac* and the model was photographed on 21 July 1865. This small portrait was displayed on Dodgson's mantelpiece at Christ Church throughout the rest of his life.

On 10 April 1867 Dodgson saw two paintings by Thomas Heaphy, 'one called *Writing to Papa*, a child lying on the floor, using a small portmanteau as a desk, the other of General Fairfax in flight, resting in a shed, with his little daughter lying fainting on his knee: her head and flowing yellow hair, against a dark blue background'.[19] This latter painting Dodgson described as 'very lovely'. Following his usual practice, a few days later Dodgson called on Heaphy to make his acquaintance. He noted on 23 April 1867: 'He received me very kindly, and we had a long and interesting talk, in spite of his being so deaf that he has to carry an ear-trumpet.'[20] Thomas Heaphy was known for his pictures depicting ghosts and apparitions, a topic that Dodgson was also interested in. Dodgson went on to report: 'He showed me also a most interesting collection of copies he has made from the earliest and most authentic portraits of Our Saviour. He is going to publish a book on the subject.' Heaphy did not live to see *The Likeness of Christ* published, but a number of friends, including Dodgson and John Ruskin, helped to get it published posthumously in 1880. On 4 April 1868, during a further visit to Heaphy's studio, Dodgson saw 'a beautiful picture he is sending to the Royal Academy of a child making the tea for breakfast, to be called *It's only Singing*. I got him to undertake to paint for me a repetition (with some necessary modifications) of the fainting child in his picture of last year.'[21] The picture was eventually entitled *Dreaming of Fairy-land*. Dodgson also acquired another picture by Heaphy of an infant St Cecilia, and both paintings were completed in April 1869.

One of Heaphy's daughters, Theodosia ('Theo'), was an artist in her own right, and she studied at Thomas Heatherley's Newman Street Studio in London, where Dodgson often visited her. Heatherley offered his studio to members of the general public wishing to study art, including life-classes and costume modelling. Many women attended the studio, but the nude life-classes were available to men only. Dodgson occasionally borrowed costumes from Heatherley for photographic purposes.[22] On 21 December 1881, Dodgson recorded: 'I went to Mr. Heatherley's, about 11, and stayed talking to Theo Heaphy, partly watching her draw, partly trying my own hand, partly watching some dozen students painting from "the life" – a handsome Egyptian girl in gorgeous robes – till about 1.'[23]

Dodgson was keen to support new artists, particularly young women, and he even paid for them to study. He had sufficient disposable income from the profits he received from the sale of the *Alice* books to spend on such philanthropic activities. For example, a neighbour's daughter, Lucy Walters, painted two of Dodgson's nieces, Nella and Violet. Dodgson wrote to thank her for the picture on 3 May 1887 and added: 'Thinking over what we said about your work, and how you would like to do some with Mr Herkomer, it occurred to me how *I* would like to treat you (if you will allow me) to a term or two of study with him, at Bushey.'[24] Lucy Walters was then aged 31 and without the financial means to pay for such tuition, and she accepted Dodgson's offer. Hubert von Herkomer

18. Edward Wakeling (ed.), *Lewis Carroll's Diaries*, vol. 5, Luton, 1999, p. 89. The fact that Dodgson felt confident enough to offer artistic advice to a painter reveals his own growing experience in artistic technique and his well-developed visual eye.

19. Ibid., p. 219.

20. Ibid., pp. 229–30.

21. Edward Wakeling (ed.), *Lewis Carroll's Diaries*, vol. 6, Clifford, 2001, pp. 14–15.

22. Edward Wakeling (ed.), *Lewis Carroll's Diaries*, vol. 7, Clifford, 2003, p. 388.

23. Ibid.

Charles L. Dodgson
Arthur Hughes and Agnes, 12 October 1863

opened an art-school at his home at Bushey, Hertfordshire, in November 1883, taking students on a termly basis. He was himself an accomplished artist and portrait painter. After Dodgson's death, his friends at Christ Church commissioned Herkomer to paint a portrait of Dodgson, based on photographs, which now hangs in the Dining Hall at the college.

Dodgson also worked with illustrators such as John Tenniel and Henry Holiday, both artists in their own right. He was conscious of the importance of illustrations in his books for children, and he knew that a good illustrator would generate positive reviews and help sales. The work of an experienced illustrator would support the text, giving visual expression to his narrative. Although his own artistic abilities were developed through the medium of photography, he did try his hand at drawing from time to time, and sketch-books of his attempts survive. However, he was never really satisfied with his own draughtsmanship, and many of his drawings were destroyed. By nature, Dodgson was inquisitive about the world around him, and he aimed to become as competent as possible in all his interests and activities – he was no passive observer. He gained experience by visiting artists in their studios, talking and discussing technique with them, and eventually offering his own advice as an art critic. He enjoyed being part of the art community – it appealed to his creative instincts and was a foil to the formal mathematical career he adopted. He was known among the Victorian artistic fraternity as a friend, patron, and supporter.

above: Charles L. Dodgson
William Holman Hunt and Cyril, 24 July 1865

opposite top left: Charles L. Dodgson
Assisted self-portrait, May or June 1856

top right: Charles L. Dodgson
Alexander Munro, June 1858

bottom left: Charles L. Dodgson
The Four Rossettis, 7 October 1863

bottom right: Charles L. Dodgson
Photograph of Minnie Morton by Sophie Anderson, July 1866

24. MS: Jon Lindseth Collection, Cleveland, Ohio.

above: Charles L. Dodgson
Agnes Hughes asleep on a couch,
12 October 1863

right: Charles L. Dodgson
Agnes Hughes standing in front of a wall,
12 October 1863

opposite top: Charles L. Dodgson
Amy and Agnes Hughes asleep on a couch,
12 October 1863

opposite bottom: Charles L. Dodgson
Agnes Hughes wearing an embroidered dress
and reclining on a couch, 12 October 1863

Charles L. Dodgson
Mary Millais in 'Waking', 21 July 1865

right: Sir John Everett Millais
Waking, 1865

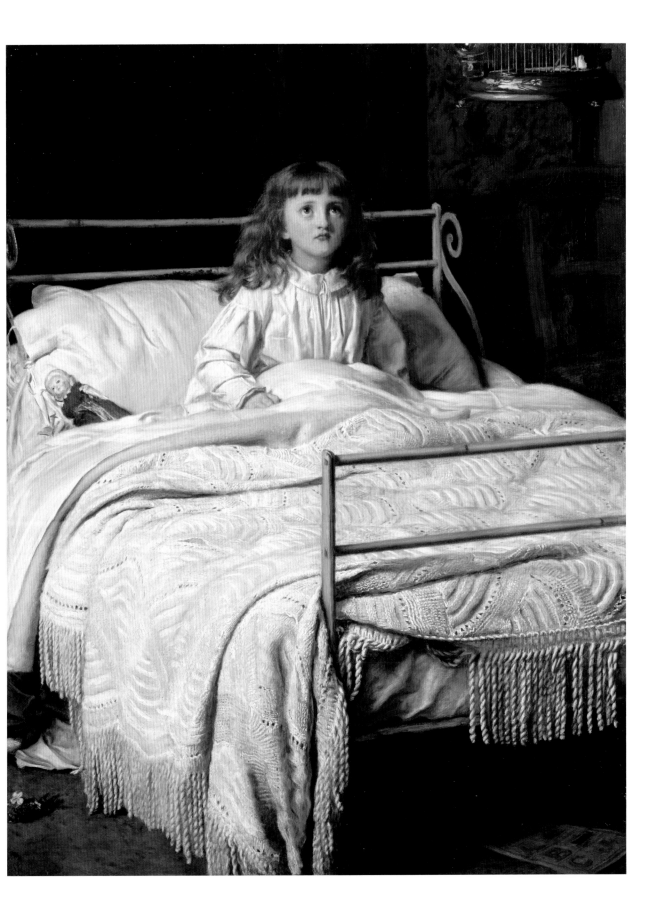

Arthur Hughes
Portrait of Mrs Leathart and Her Three Children, 1863–66

right: Arthur Hughes
The Lady with the Lilacs, 1863

51

William Holman Hunt
The Triumph of the Innocents, 1883-84

Charles L. Dodgson
The New Book, July/August 1857

George Dunlop Leslie
Alice in Wonderland, 1879

Alberto Manguel

The Universal Dream Child

'There ought to be a book written about me,
that there ought!'
Alice's Adventures in Wonderland, Chapter IV

Some time in 1884, Nathaniel Hawthorne noted in his diary: 'To write a dream, which shall resemble the real course of a dream, with all its inconsistency, its eccentricities and aimlessness – with nevertheless a leading idea running through the whole. Up to this old age of the world, no such thing has ever been written.'[1] The history of literature is made up of unexpected pairings and also failed encounters. Unbeknown to Hawthorne, the text he had deemed impossible had come into being some twenty-two years earlier, on 'a golden afternoon' of 1862, invented 'as we go along' by the Reverend Charles Lutwidge Dodgson, at the request of three young sisters, somewhere between Folly Bridge near Oxford and the sleepy village of Godstow. Because Alice's adventures are many things but, above all, they are a dream.

The historical facts of the story's telling offer a number of tempting interpretations, allowing us to imagine Alice's journey as a spiritual voyage from Folly (Bridge) to Divine Wisdom (Godstow), or a sublimation of an adult's desire for a pre-pubescent child; as a puritan's satire on Victorian mores, or as a mathematician's play on logic and the strictures of language. No doubt such readings (and many more) are conceivable. And yet overriding them all is Alice's dream.

'Alice was beginning to get very tired of sitting with her sister on the bank, and of having nothing to do', the story begins, and goes on to say that 'the hot day made her feel very sleepy and stupid'. Fatigue and drowsiness prepare the reader for the dream that will not end with Alice's first waking: it will start again with the next set of adventures, in yet another imaginary landscape that, on the last page, will perversely mirror all previous dreams and project them into the future. Somewhere towards the middle of *Through the Looking-Glass*, Tweedledee warns Alice that the Red King is dreaming of her and that she is 'only a sort of thing in his dream'. Waking at last from her own dream at the end of the second book, Alice addresses her kitten: 'Now, Kitty,' she says, 'let's consider who it was that dreamed it all … You see, Kitty, it *must* have been either me or the Red King. He was part of my dream, of course – but then I was part of his dream, too!' The reader is left with this appalling supposition.

Alice's dreams bring to mind those of an earlier dreamer and traveller, who tells us that he was 'so full of sleep' when he lost his way in the dark wood, halfway along the road of life. Dante's adventures, however, are not dreamlike in the same way as Alice's; on the contrary, his otherworldly realms have the imaginative solidity of atrociously real places and his theological geographies are too exact for a dreamer to become lost in. The fact is that stories framed by dreams are not usually successful as dreams. The explicit slumbers of Bunyan's Christian or Morris's John Ball, or the less explicit ones of Proust's Marcel and Joyce's Finnegan, read true as allegories and fables, or as musing reverie

1. Nathaniel Hawthorne, 'The American Notebooks', in *The Portable Hawthorne*, ed. Malcolm Cowley, Harmondsworth: Penguin, 1977, p. 628.

and nightmarish wordplay, but not as dreams. Alice's Wonderland, instead, is told in an altogether different state of mind, both aimless and rigorously structured, as Hawthorne demanded. It obeys no conventional material rules but transforms itself constantly into something else, through a kind of nightmarish logic. 'How puzzling all these changes are!' Alice mildly observes, falling down the rabbit-hole and winding her way through mad rooms and impossible gardens.

As Alice quickly discovers, all paths in Wonderland lead to madness, or at least to that state which Carroll himself, in a diary entry dated 9 February 1856, defined as 'an inability to distinguish which is the waking and which the sleeping life'. 'We often dream without the least suspicion of unreality',[2] he wrote, perfectly describing Alice's condition. For Alice the dream is real, as dreams are to the dreamer, and the places she visits and the people she meets should (but don't) obey the logic of her waking world. 'When I used to read fairy tales,' she says to herself, her suddenly gigantic body crammed in the Rabbit's house, 'I fancied that kind of thing never happened, and now I am in the middle of one!' Indeed she is, and here, as she retains the mind of her waking, sane self, madness must be that which now surrounds her; it is the others who are mad, a safety which the Cheshire Cat soon shatters: 'We're all mad here. I'm mad. You're mad. … You must be,' it tells her, 'or you wouldn't have come here.' The state of dream-madness is horribly proven by the very fact that she is dreaming it.

I suspect that much of the power of the *Alice* books comes from the fact that the dreams she inhabits are 'as large as life, and twice as natural'. If her dreams are nonsense, they are natural nonsense, or at least nonsense that seems natural for her, albeit objectionable, and therefore believable for the readers who realise that Wonderland and the Looking-Glass universe secretly reflect their own perception of the world's madness. Greedy financiers repeat the Hatter's injunction of 'No room!' when there is plenty of room;

tyrannical politicians copy the Duchess's admonition that we have as much right to think 'as pigs have to fly'; prejudiced public opinion echoes the Queen of Hearts' demand 'Sentence first – verdict afterwards!'; consumer-driven advertisers insist, with the Mock Turtle, that we too 'join the dance'. All are recognisable inhabitants of Wonderland, but also of our realms, too close to home for comfort.

Alice's dream worlds echo through much of the literature that follows Carroll's books, and also reflect back to the literature that preceded them, which can be read differently after Alice. Borges once suggested that every writer creates his own precursors. For a reader of the *Alice* books, certain episodes of *Gulliver's Travels* (Gulliver tied down by the Lilliputians or his inspection by the Brobdingnag princess) seem to mirror Alice's own metamorphoses. Tristram Shandy's father, asking whether this is 'a fit time to talk of Pensions and Grenadiers', expands on the Walrus's observation that the time has come to talk about 'cabbages and kings'. And how curious that Polonius, fulsomely agreeing with Hamlet that a cloud is like a camel, or a weasel, or 'very like a whale', is the exact reverse of the Red Queen, who disagrees with Alice on principle: 'When you say "hill",' she tells Alice, 'I could show you hills, in comparison with which you'd call that a valley.' A rich anthology could be compiled of Alice's ancestors: Ulysses calling himself Nobody among the Cyclops is like Alice saying 'Who am I then? Tell me that first, and then, if I like being that person, I'll come up; if not I'll stay down here till I'm somebody else'; Tweedledum and Tweedledee, battling until the end of time over their rattle, are Cain and Abel, and Joseph and any one of his many siblings, and Alexandre Dumas's Corsican brothers, and the ongoing duellists portrayed by Joseph Conrad in his story; Don Quixote, sad and clumsy like the White Knight; Salome resembling a younger version of the Queen of Hearts and clamouring 'Off with his head!'

2. *Lewis Carroll's Diaries: The Private Journals of Charles Lutwidge Dodgson*, vol. 2, ed. Edward Wakeling, Luton: The Lewis Carroll Society, 2007.

In our own time, Alice's dream world is as much part of our literary *imaginaire* as Ulysses's travels or Don Quixote's jousts. It seeps into Kafka's bureaucratic nightmares, and colours his *Trial* with that of the King's Messenger ('He's in prison now, being punished: and the trial doesn't even begin till next Wednesday: and of course the crime comes last of all'), and his unattainable *Castle* with the White Queen's bewildering spatial rules ('Now, *here*, you see, it takes all the running *you* can do, to keep in the same place!'). It is not inconceivable that Kafka, Carroll's near contemporary, might have read *Alice* in the first German translation, by Antoine Zimmermann, published in 1869, almost half a century before his own dream of transformation, *The Metamorphosis*, was published. 'I wonder if I've been changed in the night?' is Alice's version of Kafka's terrible first line: 'Upon waking from troubled dreams, Gregor Samsa found himself changed into a giant insect.'

Alice and her troubled dreams inhabit so much of our literature that it is impossible to compile a comprehensive catalogue in a few pages. Detective fiction (Fredric Brown's *Night of the Jabberwock*), science fiction (Roger Zelazny's *Sign of Chaos*), philosophy (Gilles Deleuze's *Logic of Sense*), horror fiction (Graham Masterton's *Mirror*), logic (Francis Huxley's *The Raven and the Writing Desk*) are all steeped in the *Alice* books, as are G.K. Chesterton's *The Man Who Was Thursday*, Paul Auster's *City of Glass*, Percival Everett's *The Water Cure*, Julián Ríos's *Sombreros para Alicia* [*Hats for Alice*], Joyce Carol Oates's *Wonderland*, Haruki Murakami's *A Wild Sheep Chase*.

In 1922, Vladimir Nabokov translated *Alice* into Russian and allowed himself a Carrollian freedom in his version, which is considered to be the best translation of *Alice* into any language. Alice herself became Anya, while the French mouse who came over with William the Conqueror was turned into a mouse left over after Napoleon's retreat. According to the biographer Brian Boyd,[3] Nabokov's story 'Invitation to a Beheading', written twelve years later, shows the influence of Carroll's work, except that while in Nabokov's text language remains logical, in Carroll's it escapes the boundaries of common sense and insists in being its literal self: 'I see nobody on the road,' says Alice. To which the King answers: 'I only wish *I* had such eyes … To be able to see Nobody! And at that distance too!'

Commenting on the Wonderland adventures, Nabokov noted that, if Carroll's text is read very carefully, it 'will be seen to imply, by humorous juxtaposition, the presence of a quite solid, and rather sentimental, world, behind the semi-detached dream'.[4] This perceptive observation defines Nabokov's own work as well: it is precisely that underlying material world that sustains his masterpiece *Pale Fire*, in which the dreamlike poem by the inspired John Shade (where Carroll's Red King makes a ghostly appearance) allows or implies the mock-academic, 'solid' and 'sentimental' commentary of the pompous Charles Kinbote. After we have read *Pale Fire*, the strict, unjust, prejudiced Victorian world appears even more clearly through the translucent madness of Alice's dream worlds.

Perhaps of all the major contemporary writers who acknowledged their debt to Alice, Jorge Luis Borges was the most explicit. Borges read the *Alice* books in English during his Buenos Aires childhood, and the darker, more troubling aspects of the adventures inspired many of his own metaphysical reflections, and games with time and the labyrinths of space. 'Both of Alice's dreams,' wrote Borges in an introduction to a so-called *Complete Works of Lewis Carroll* in Spanish, 'continually border the nightmare. Tenniel's illustrations (now inherent to the work, and which Carroll disliked) accentuate the always suggested menace. At first sight or in our recollection, the adventures seem arbitrary and almost irresponsible; then we see that they hold the secret rigour of chess and card-games, which are also adventures of the imagination.'[5]

3. Brian Boyd, *Vladimir Nabokov: The Russian Years*, Princeton: Princeton University Press, 1990, p. 415.
4. Cited in Boyd, *Vladimir Nabokov*, p. 414.
5. Jorge Luis Borges, 'Prólogo a Lewis Carroll, *Obras Completas*, tomo II', in Borges, *Prólogos con un Prólogo de prólogos*, Buenos Aires: Torres Agüero Editor, 1975, p. 109. There is no evidence to suggest that Carroll was unhappy with the Tenniel illustrations.

This 'secret rigour' runs through 'The Garden of Forking Paths', 'An Examination of the Work of Herbert Quain', 'The Approach to al-Mu'tasim', 'Death and the Compass' and other stories in which the invisible rules of a game determine the fate of the protagonists who, like Alice, do not know that they are playing it. In all, the intention of the plot seems one thing, the result is seen to be another. Just like the logical unfolding of the events in Wonderland's maze of apparent nonsense, in Borges's fictions too absurdity is only the appearance of the story: a man wishing to kill another for no evident reason, a writer trying to include all of literature in his work, a seeker of the truth failing to recognise the bearer of that truth, a detective unravelling the mystery of a murder which he does not know is his own. Borges's reader has to wait to be told why such things happen; in Wonderland or the Looking-Glass world, Alice can ask the gardeners why they are painting the roses red, argue about the validity of the King's rules in court, insist that Humpty-Dumpty explain himself, put an end to the mad card trial and the mad chess banquet by confronting the perpetrators. Borges's protagonists suffer their dreams and become their victims; Alice, more wisely, understands that things in a dream must be challenged and does so triumphantly.

Borges wondered whether Carroll was aware of the ultimately horrible fate of his heroine, condemned to wander through a world incomprehensible to her but not to others, and he suspected that Carroll must have felt, perhaps unconsciously, that Alice's estranged universe was not unlike his own. For that reason, Borges noted that the most unforgettable of the episodes in the *Alice* books was, for him, her farewell to the White Knight. 'Perhaps the Knight is moved,' Borges says, 'because he knows that he is Alice's dream, just as Alice was a dream of the Red King, and that he is about to vanish. The Knight is also Lewis Carroll, bidding farewell to the dear dreams that inhabited his loneliness.'[6]

Tweedledee's awful question to Alice concerning the Red King's dream ('And if he left off dreaming about you…') is the epigraph to one of Borges's most celebrated stories, 'The Circular Ruins', in which a man manages to dream another man into the world, only to discover that he himself is a dream. This story, with its roots in the Looking-Glass world, was written in 1940; about the same time, Borges had read a story by the Italian writer Giovanni Papini, 'The Sick Gentleman's Last Visit', which he later included in an anthology of fantastic tales. Papini, himself a reader of Carroll, imagines a man who realises he is a dream and attempts to wake his dreamer in order to be no more. Unlike Alice, who wants to assert her existence even through tears (to which Tweedledum implacably replies: 'I hope you don't suppose those are real tears?'), the heroes of Papini and Borges come to believe in their dream condition and then want to end it. Alice is more courageous. Realising that she is indeed the stuff of dreams, she declares that she herself is responsible for the dream which she inhabits: 'It's my own invention,' she defiantly says.

We readers (vaguely aware that we too may be a dream) believe Alice, because her dreams are, in a literal sense, real. At the end of *Alice's Adventures in Wonderland*, Alice's sister picks up on Alice's dream, and as she listens, or seems to listen, 'the whole place around her became alive with the strange creatures of her little sister's dream'. What we readers follow is not Reverend Charles Dodgson's narrative', translated through the persona of Lewis Carroll. We follow Alice herself, following the White Rabbit, following the elusive Mary Ann. Like Don Quixote and his Cervantes or like Ulysses and his Homer, Alice is more alive to us than her creator. This is perhaps what Dodgson would have wished, both for himself and for his dream child.

6. Borges, 'Prólogo a Lewis Carroll', p. 111.

On which occasion I told them the fairy-tale of "Alice's Adventures Under Ground," which I undertook to write out for Alice, & which is now finished (as to the text) though the pictures are not yet nearly done — Feb. 10. 1863

nor yet — Mar. 12. 1864.

"Alice's Hour in Elfland"? June 9/64.
"Alice's Adventures in Wonderland"? June 28.

July 4 (F) Atkinson brought over to my rooms some friends of his, a Mrs & Miss Peters, of whom I took photographs, & who afterwards looked over my albums & staid to lunch. They then went off to the Museum, & Duckworth & I made an expedition up the river to Godstow with the 3 Liddells: we had tea on the bank there, & did not reach Ch. Ch. again till ¼ past 8, when we took them on to my rooms to see my collection of micro-photographs, & restored them to the Deanery, just before 9

July 5 (Sat.) Left, with Atkinson, for London at 9..2, meeting at the station the Liddells, who went by the same train. We reached 4. Alfred Place about 11, & found Aunt L. P.J., & E.L. there, & took the 2 last to see Marochetti's studio. After luncheon Atkinson left, & we visited the International Bazaar.

Pages from Dodgson's diaries, volume 8
9 May 1862 – 6 September 1864

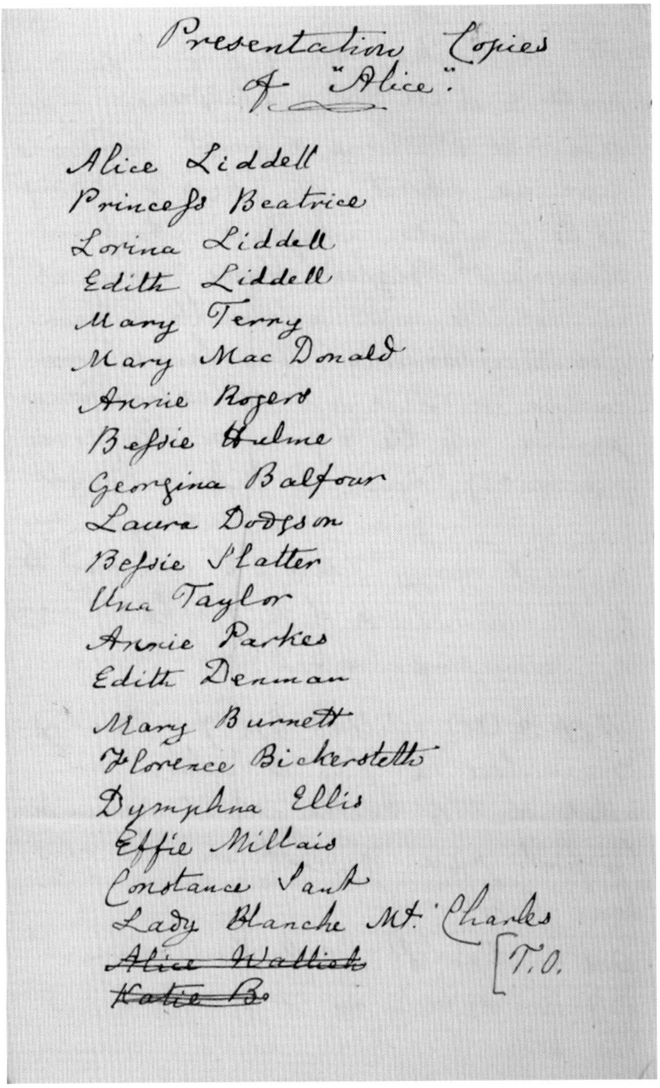

Presentation Copies of "Alice":

Alice Liddell
Princess Beatrice
Lorina Liddell
Edith Liddell
Mary Terry
Mary Mac Donald
Annie Rogers
Bessie Hulme
Georgina Balfour
Laura Dodgson
Bessie Slatter
Una Taylor
Annie Parkes
Edith Denman
Mary Burnett
Florence Bickersteth
Dymphna Ellis
Effie Millais
Constance Saut
Lady Blanche M. Charles
~~Alice Wattick~~   [T.O.
~~Katie B.~~

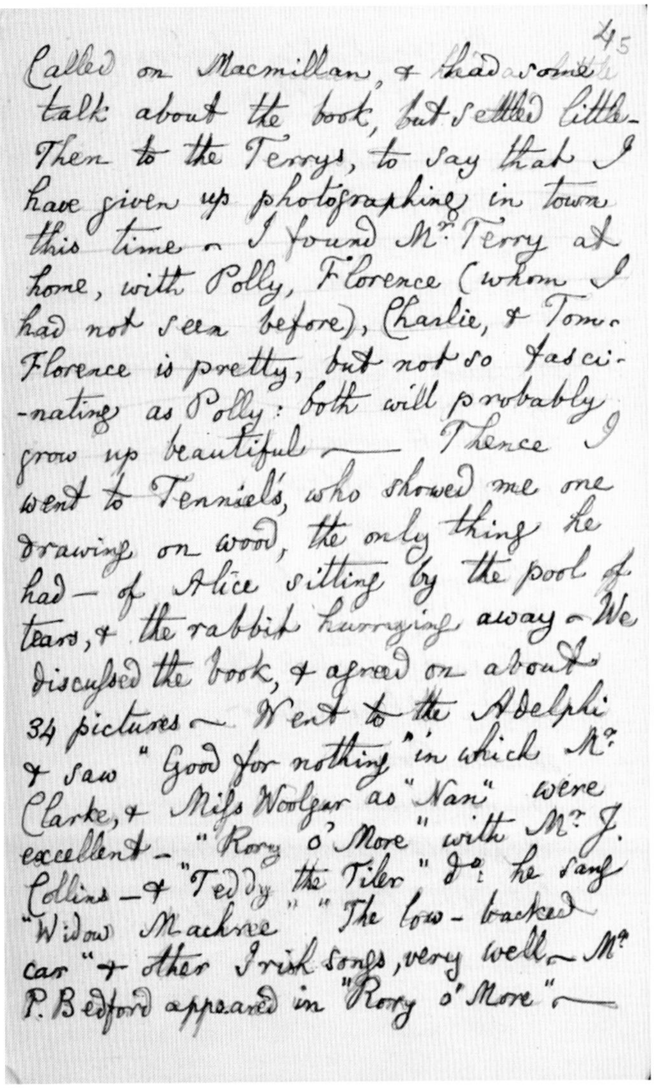

Called on Macmillan, & thadavonett talk about the book, but settled little. Then to the Terrys, to say that I have given up photographing in town this time ~ I found M. Terry at home, with Polly, Florence (whom I had not seen before), Charlie, & Tom. Florence is pretty, but not so fascinating as Polly: both will probably grow up beautiful —— Thence I went to Tenniel's, who showed me one drawing on wood, the only thing he had — of Alice sitting by the pool of tears, & the rabbit hurrying away ~ We discussed the book, & agreed on about 34 pictures ~ Went to the Adelphi & saw "Good for nothing" in which M. Clarke, & Miss Woolgar as "Nan" were excellent — "Rory o' More" with M. J. Collins — & "Teddy the Tiler" do. he sang "Widow Machree" "The low-backed car" & other Irish songs, very well — M. P. Bedford appeared in "Rory o' More" —

Pages from Dodgson's diaries, volume 9
13 September 1864 – 24 January 1868

Charles L. Dodgson
Original drawing - sketch of Alice with Ostrich

top right: Charles L. Dodgson
Original drawing – sketches of heads (including Alice)

bottom right: Charles L. Dodgson
Original drawing of rabbits

Charles L. Dodgson
Original drawing of the Pool of Tears

top right: Charles L. Dodgson
Original drawing - sketch of the caterpiller

bottom right: Charles L. Dodgson
Original drawing of Giant Puppy

B. 12

Chapter 1

Alice was beginning to get very tired of sitting by her sister on the bank, and of having nothing to do: once or twice she had peeped into the book her sister was reading, but it had no pictures or conversations in it, and where is the use of a book, thought Alice, without pictures or conversations? So she was considering in her own mind, (as well as she could, for the hot day made her feel very sleepy and stupid,) whether the pleasure of making a daisy-chain was worth the trouble of getting up and picking the daisies, when a white rabbit with pink eyes ran close by her.

There was nothing very remarkable in that, nor did Alice think it so very much out of the way to hear the rabbit say to itself "dear, dear! I shall be too late!" (when she thought it over afterwards, it occurred to her that she ought to have wondered at this, but at the time it all seemed quite natural); but when the rabbit actually took a watch out of its waistcoat-pocket, looked at it, and then hurried on, Alice started to her feet, for

2

A Christmas Gift to a Dear Child in Memory of a Summer Day.

Charles L. Dodgson
Alice's Adventures under Ground, 1864

right: Charles L. Dodgson
Draft title page for *Alice's Adventures in Wonderland*

A 14

ALICE'S ADVENTURES IN WONDERLAND.

BY

LEWIS CARROLL.

WITH TWENTY-FOUR ILLUSTRATIONS BY

JOHN TENNIELL.

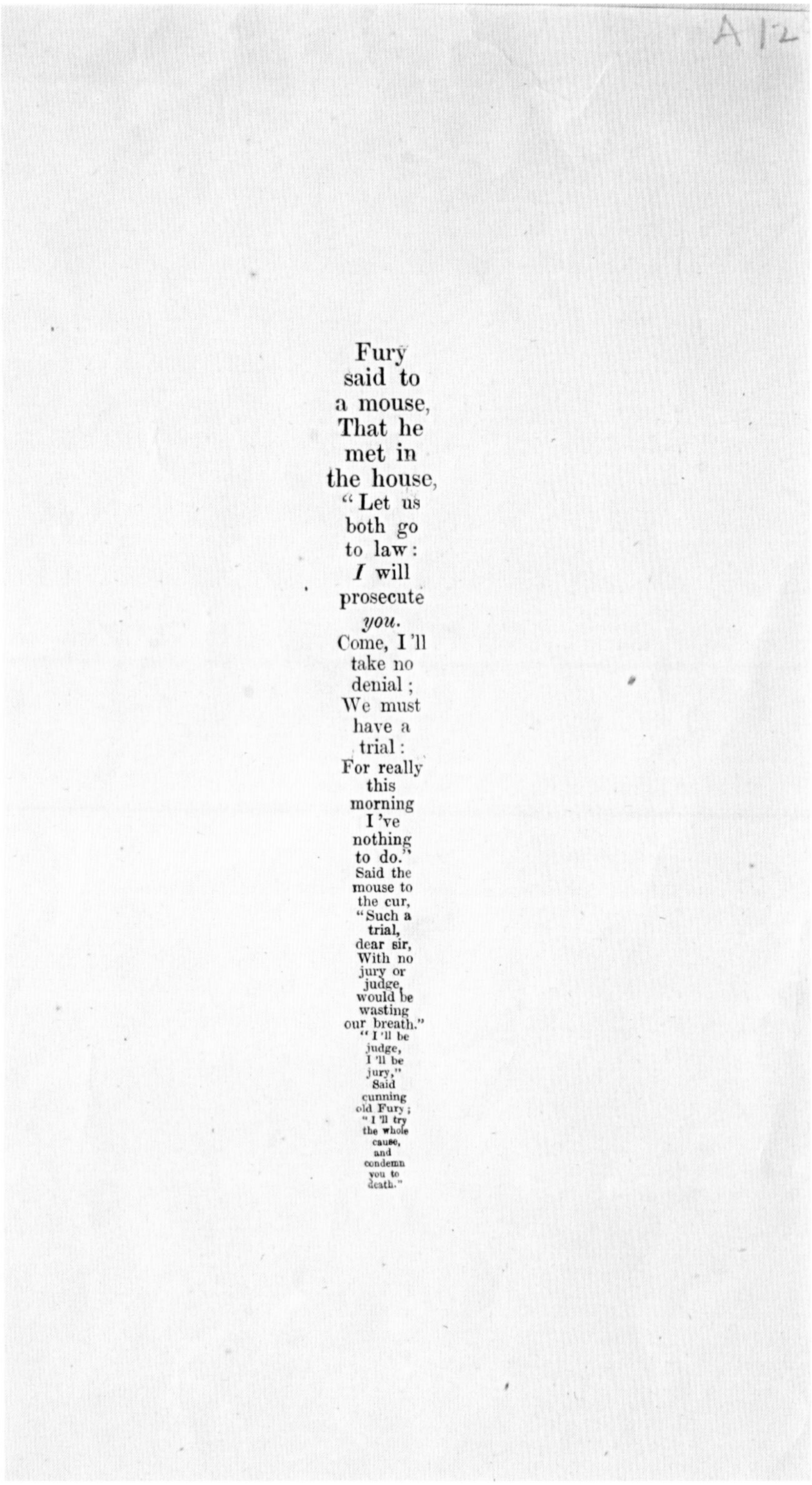

A 12

Fury
said to
a mouse,
That he
met in
the house,
" Let us
both go
to law :
I will
prosecute
you.
Come, I 'll
take no
denial ;
We must
have a
trial :
For really
this
morning
I 've
nothing
to do."
Said the
mouse to
the cur,
"Such a
trial,
dear sir,
With no
jury or
judge,
would be
wasting
our breath."
" I 'll be
judge,
I 'll be
jury,"
Said
cunning
old Fury ;
" I 'll try
the whole
cause,
and
condemn
you to
death."

Charles L. Dodgson
Proof sheet of the straight version of the Mouse's Tale
from the Macmillan printed edition.

right: Charles L. Dodgson
Proof sheet of the Mouse's Tail, cut up and re-pasted
by Dodgson in a curve.

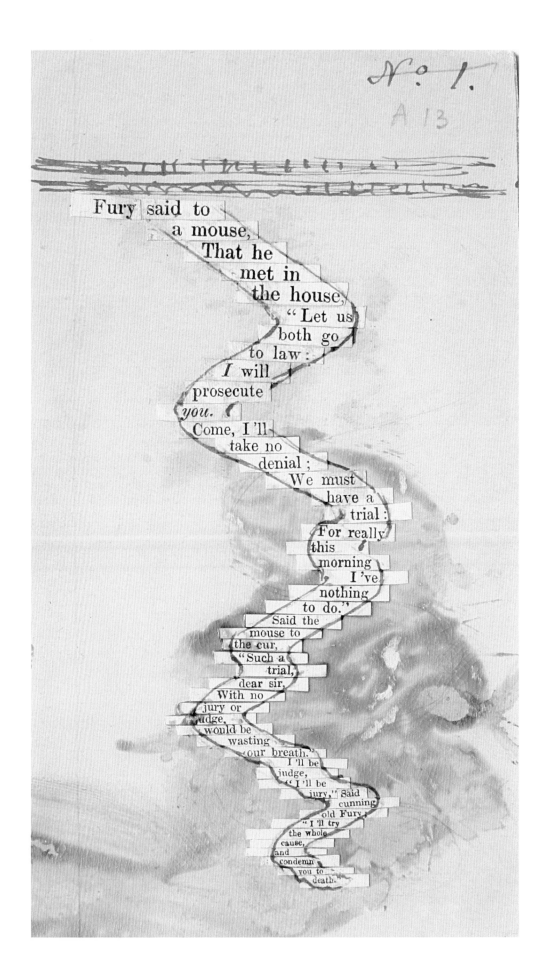

Fury said to
a mouse,
That he
met in
the house,
"Let us
both go
to law :
I will
prosecute
you.
Come, I'll
take no
denial ;
We must
have a
trial :
For really
this
morning
I've
nothing
to do."
Said the
mouse to
the cur,
"Such a
trial,
dear sir,
With no
jury or
judge,
would be
wasting
our breath."
I'll be
judge,
"I'll be
jury," Said
cunning
old Fury
"I'll try
the whole
cause,
and
condemn
you to
death."

CHAPTER I.

DOWN THE RABBIT-HOLE.

ALICE was beginning to get very tired of sitting by her sister on the bank, and of having nothing to do : once or twice she had peeped into the book her sister was reading, but it had no pictures or conversations in it, " and what is

above: Charles L. Dodgson
Proof sheet for *Alice in Wonderland* Macmillan printed edition with additional drawing.

right: Charles L. Dodgson
Proof sheet from 1886 facsimile edition of the manuscript of *Alice's Adventures under Ground*.

dried her eyes to
see what was coming.
It was the white
rabbit coming back
again, splendidly
dressed, with a
pair of white kid
gloves in one hand,
and a nosegay in
the other. Alice was ready to ask help of any
one, she felt so desperate, and as the rabbit
passed her, she said, in a low, timid voice,
"If you please, Sir ___ " the rabbit started
violently, looked up once into the roof of
the hall, from which the voice seemed to come,
and then dropped the nosegay and the white
kid gloves, and skurried away into the dark.
-ness as hard as it could go.

Alice took up the nosegay and gloves,
and found the nosegay so delicious that
she kept smelling at it all the time she
went on talking to herself ___ "dear, dear!
how queer everything is today! and yester-
-day everything happened just as usual:
I wonder if I was changed in the night?
Let me think: was I the same when I
got up this morning? I think I remember

13

$\varepsilon =$ ordered to be electrotyped   p. 23

8 × ε Jabberwock — [full-page] — ~~Frontispiece~~
     Frontispiece of Alice and Knight.

1 × ε Black Kitten   [3 × 2]   p. 1   (4)

2 × ε Alice in arm-chair [3½ × 2¼]   p. 5   (6)
     w × 12 29

3 × ε Looking-glass ——— [d°]   p. 11   (1)

4 × ε   d°   ——— [d°]   12   (2)

5 × ε Chess men in hearth [w × 2¾]   14   (3)
     12 13

6 × ε King being dusted — [d°]   17
7 × ε Knight on poker — [2 × 2½]   20
9 × ε Talking flowers — [3½ × ~~2¾~~] ~~28~~ 30
10 × ε Meeting Red Queen [2¾ × 3½] ~~34~~ 34
     = 12 lines

11 × ε Chess-board — [3 × 2]   38 (or else 45)
     w × 9 10 41 40

12 × ε Running — [3½ × 2¼] ~~48~~ 46 (or else 39)
     w × 10 11½

13 × ε Railway-carriage — [3½ × 2¾] ~~48~~ ~~50~~ 49 50
     w × 12 13

14 × ε Rocking horse fly — [3 × 2] ~~55~~ 55
     w × 10

15 × ε Snap dragon fly — [3 × 2] ~~55~~ ~~57~~ 57

16 × ε Bread & butter fly — [3 × 2] ~~56~~ ~~58~~ 58

17 × ε Alice & Fawn — [2¾ × 3] 64 63
     w × 19

18 × ε Tweedledum & Tweedledee [3½ × 2¾] 64 67
     w × 19

19 × ε Walrus & Carpenter 3½ × 2¼ 68 73

20 × ε   d°   ——— d° "   74 74

21 × ε   d°   ——— d°   74 78

22 × ε Red King asleep [3 × 2]   79 80
     w × 10

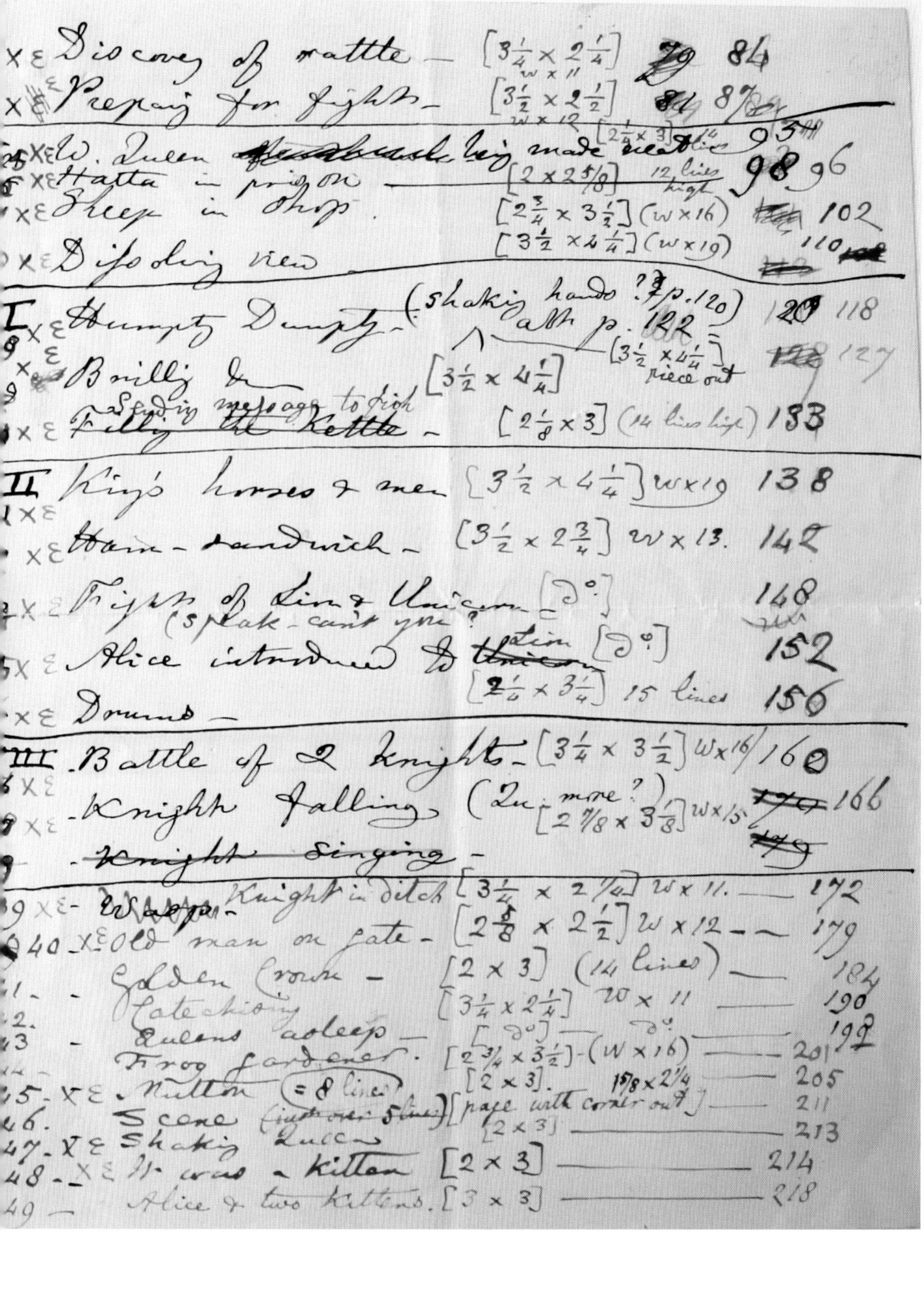

× ε Discovery of rattle — [3¼ × 2¼] ~~79~~ 84
w × 11
× ε Preparing for fight — [3½ × 2½] ~~84~~ 87
w × 12
× ε W. Queen ~~[illegible]~~ being made neat [2¼ × 3] w × 14 93
× ε Hatta in prison — [2 × 2⅝] 12 lines high 98 96
× ε Sheep in shop. [2¾ × 3½] (w × 16) ~~106~~ 102
× ε Dissolving view [3½ × 4¼] (w × 19) ~~113~~ 110
I × ε Humpty Dumpty — (shaking hands ? p. 120) alt p. 122 [3½ × 4¼ piece out] ~~120~~ 118
× ε Brillig &c [3½ × 4¼] ~~126~~ 127
× ε ~~Filling the Kettle~~ sending message to fish — [2⅛ × 3] (14 lines high) 133
II King's horses & men [3½ × 4¼] w × 19 138
× ε Ham-sandwich — [3½ × 2¾] w × 13. 142
× ε Fight of Lion & Unicorn — [D°] 148
(speak — can't you?)
× ε Alice introduces ~~Unicorn~~ Lion [D°] 152
× ε Drums — [2¼ × 3¼] 15 lines 156
III Battle of 2 Knights — [3¼ × 3½] w × 16 160
× ε Knight falling (2 more?) [2⅞ × 3⅛] w × 15 ~~170~~ 166
~~Knight singing~~ — ~~170~~
39 × ε ~~Wasp~~ Knight in ditch [3¼ × 2¼] w × 11. — 172
40 × ε Old man on gate — [2⅝ × 2½] w × 12 — 179
41 — Golden Crown — [2 × 3] (14 lines) — 184
42. — Catechising [3¼ × 2¼] w × 11 — 190
43 — Queens asleep — [D°] — D° — 192
44 — Frog gardener. [2¾ × 3½] — (w × 16) — 201
45 × ε Mutton (= 8 lines) [2 × 3]. — 205
46. Scene (instead of 5 lines) [page with corner out] 1⅝ × 2¼ — 211
47 × ε Shaking Queen [2 × 3] — 213
48 × ε It was a kitten [2 × 3] — 214
49 — Alice & two kittens. [3 × 3] — 218

top: John Tenniel
The Jabberwock with eyes of flame, 1870–71

bottom: John Tenniel
Through the looking glass, 1870-71

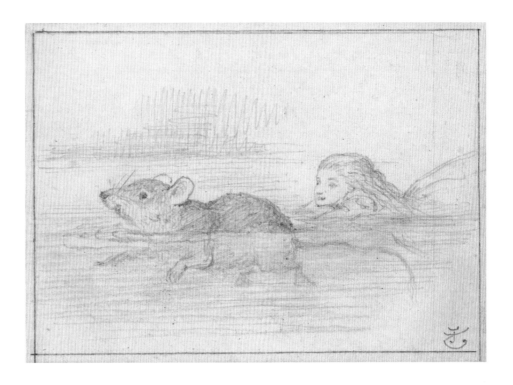

bottom: John Tenniel
Sit down, all of you, and listen to me!, 1864–65

top: John Tenniel
The Pool of Tears, 1864–65

The Wonderland

Postage-Stamp Case

PUNCH, OR THE LONDON CHARIVARI.—August 28, 1880.

LITTLE VICTIMS.

Hare (terrified). "WHAT'S THAT?—THE LORDS?"   Rabbit (shuddering). "P'R'APS IT'S THE FARMERS!!"

(With Mr. Punch's apologies to "The Princes in the Tower," by J. E. Millais, R.A.)

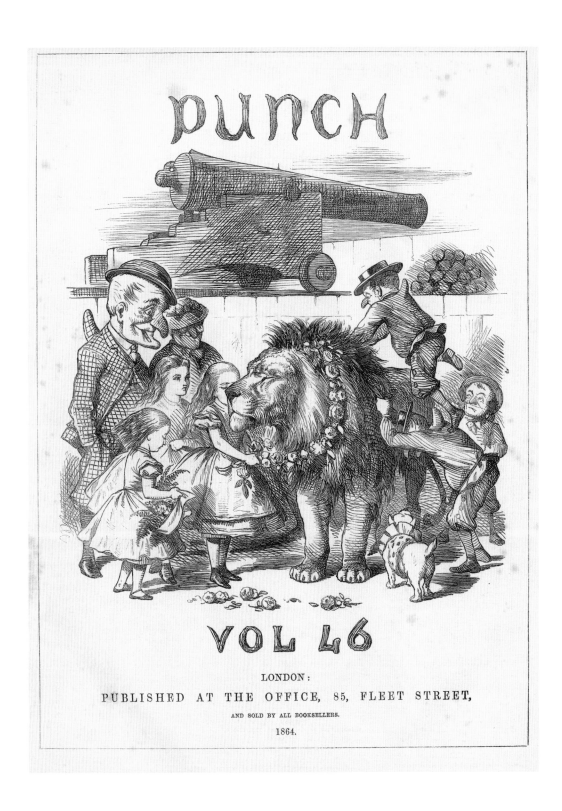

top left: The New and Diverting Game of Alice in Wonderland, 1918

bottom left: *The Wonderland Postage-Stamp Case*, 1890

left: John Tenniel
Caricature based on Tenniel's illustrations of
'Alice's Adventures in Wonderland' in *Punch* magazine,
26 February 1880

above: John Tenniel
Title page of *Punch* magazine, Vol 46, 1864

PRINCE OF WALES'S THEATRE.

ON

THURSDAY AFTERNOON, DECEMBER 23, 1886,

AND EVERY AFTERNOON,

A MUSICAL DREAM-PLAY,

Founded upon the Stories of

Mr. LEWIS CARROLL.

BOX OFFICE NOW OPEN FROM 11 TO 5.

R. O. HEARSON, Printer, 101, Leadenhall Street, E.C.

Alexander Bassano
Charles Hayden Coffin as the Mad Hatter; Estelle Dudley as Alice in 'Alice in Wonderland', 14 December 1917

left: Theatre poster of *Alice in Wonderland* in the Prince of Wales's Theatre, 1886

****

BETWEEN EATING AND LOVING AN *ALICIOUS*, ANNOTATED FAIRY TALE

CAROL MAVOR

****

1. Emmet Gowin (b. 1941 in Danville, Virginia) is an American photographer, famed for his use of the large-format camera and his 'family pictures'. *Nancy* is one of the key images in his oeuvre. Gowin's family photographs of children, like those made later by Sally Mann (b. 1951 in Lexington, Virginia), arrest the viewer, in ways different from and akin to those by Dodgson.

2. The artist elin o'Hara slavick, who happens to own a copy of *Nancy*, describes Gowin's image as follows: 'Bataille eyes of hope and desire, ovals of chance and light held lightly in her perfect hands; her head thrown back ever so slightly in joyful determination to pose just so, the crumpled white cotton nightdress just slept and woken in, country starlet bangs framing her eyes wide shut, her closed lips, that fierce youth. She fills the grassy field with spectacular energy, her body a glowing root, an immortalized girl about to feast, offering us the world.' See the online journal *Saint Lucy*: http://saint-lucy.com/one-picture-one-paragraph/elin-ohara-slavick/ (undated). Many of the Surrealists, perhaps most notably Salvador Dalí and Max Ernst, were fans of Lewis Carroll's other-worldly dream stories.

'*Between eating and loving: An Alicious, annotated fairy tale' is a retelling of the Alice 'stories' (both real and fictional), centring not on a photograph of Alice Liddell, nor any picture by Charles Dodgson (Lewis Carroll). Instead, this modern fairy tales circle its 'Once-upon-a-time' O around Emmet Gowin's 1969 photograph of Nancy (taken in Danville, Virginia).*[1] *Through Gowin's camera eye as mouth, Nancy, with her serpentine arms, offers the viewer eggs (as an after-image of St. Lucy's eyes). In my Alicious story (as suggested by Humpty Dumpty as inferred by Georges Bataille's* Story of the Eye[2]*), eggs exist in that uneasy place between eating and loving, like a Dodgson photograph of Alice, like a Gowin photograph of Nancy.*

Let's pretend.

It is the 4th of July 1969.

Virginia.

*O*nce again (not 'Once upon a time'), there is a charming little girl.[3]

Seven-year-old Nancy truly loves nothing better than two poached eggs on toast. She likes them best served with a side of fried green tomatoes and a big dollop of white grits, with a pond of melting yellow butter in the centre.[4]

'*O*'s of eggs; an '*O*' of grits with a little '*o*' of butter, and three or four '*O*'s of green tomatoes: such a feast feeds Nancy's morning *oralia*.[5]

But what Nancy likes better than poached eggs on toast is golden custard, specifically Julia Child's *crème renversée au caramel*. Nancy developed a taste for fancy cooking through her mother, an outstanding cook, who learned to 'cook French' in New Orleans. Nancy loves to watch the final step of *crème renversée au caramel*: the moment when her mother turns the shiny yellow custard upside down, flipping it over, so the top becomes the bottom and the burnt-sugar-caramel bottom becomes the extra-delicious top.[6]

A plate to feed Nancy's morning *auralia*.[7]

When Nancy's mother makes Julia Child's *crème renversée au caramel*, she saves the unneeded egg whites for the Reverend to make albumen for his photographic prints.[8] The Reverend is a great amateur photographer. Their little town in Virginia is the Reverend's 'Storyville'; the Reverend has the butterfly touch of E.J. Bellocq.[9]

Nancy's family have their own glazed hen house.[10] When Nancy's mother is in the mood for making Julia Child's *crème renversée au caramel*, she sends Nancy out to the hen house to gather fresh eggs

When Nancy is not 'hangin about' with 'mama', she is often with her friend, the 'Revrin', who is very interested in the culinary (and somewhat poisonous) aspects of old-time photographic

3. This fairy tale, which takes place on the 4th of July 1969, is a *double* to the original story of Alice, which was first told to the real Alice (Alice Liddell) by the Reverend Charles Dodgson on the 4th of July 1862. Lewis Carroll was, of course, the literary double of Dodgson.

Doubling is inherent to Dodgson the man (he was famously author, mathematician, logician, deacon, Oxford don, photographer and inventor), as well as to the complex literary play of Carroll's *Alice's Adventures in Wonderland* and *Through the Looking-glass*. Doublings, in *both* the Alice books, are endless. Perhaps the most obvious doubles are Tweedledum and Tweedledee. The White Rabbit, the Dodo, the White Knight and Alice herself have all been read as character doubles of Dodgson. Alice, too, is often shown as a double: for example, she once tried to 'box her own ears for having cheated herself in a game of croquet she was playing against herself ... [for Alice] was very fond of pretending to be two people' (*The Annotated Alice: The Definitive Edition: Alice's Adventures in Wonderland and Through the Looking-glass*, introduction and notes by Martin Gardner, New York and London: W.W. Norton, 2000, p. 18). At the heart of such doubling is the fact that twoness is the very essence of the photograph, a coupling of reality and fiction: made from a negative printed into a positive, where one negative reproduces endless 'doubles'. Not to be overlooked here either is Carroll's coinage of the literary 'portmanteau word': two words packed into one. The portmanteau *slithy* (explained by Humpty Dumpty as being formed from 'lithe' and 'slimy') is like the suitcase of the same name, but rather than being two bags in one, it is two words in one.

As has been often noted, photography fed Carroll's literary work, especially *Through the Looking-glass*, a mise en abyme of dreams within dreams, which plays on the *photographicness* of Alice's encounters (the endless doubles and variables of 'realness'). In its early days, photography was referred to as 'Daguerre's mirror', in reference to one of the medium's pioneers, Louis Daguerre (1787–1851). Daguerre invented the 'daguerreotype', the first commercially successful form of photography, whose surface is like a mirror.

4. Grits (coarsely ground cornmeal) is a bland, regional dish peculiar to the American South. It is fundamental to (and meto-nymical of) the culture, not unlike England's 'tea and biscuits'.

5. The large letter 'O', which often begins the fairy tale, with great ornamental flurry, is derived from the Egyptian hieroglyph for the eye: both the iris and the pupil are circles. Yet an 'O' is also an open mouth. Furthermore, both the eye and the mouth ingest as figures of *oralia*. *Oralia* is a term invented by Michael Moon to describe Joseph Cornell's art (with its emphases on childhood and fairy-tale themes) and the artist's peculiar taste for childish sweets. As Moon points out, while *oralia* emphasises the double consumption of the mouth and the eye, it is also a variant of the Latin *auralia*, which means golden. See Michael Moon, *A Small Boy and Others: Imitation and Initiation in American Culture from Henry James to Andy Warhol*, Durham and London: Duke University Press, 1998, p. 138.

Alice's Adventures in Wonderland is a once-upon-a-time story that emphasises eating; it was, of course, told on an *aurelian* – 'golden' – afternoon, as is stated in the prefatory verse of the book. The verse begins as follows: 'All in the golden afternoon / Full leisurely we glide; / For both our oars, with little skill, / By little arms are plied, / While little hands make vain pretence / Our wanderings to guide' (*The Annotated Alice*, p. 7).

6. *Crème renversée au caramel* evokes the reversal of the photographic process during Dodgson's time. Using a photographer's black cloth over his head and the back of the camera, Dodgson would have seen his subjects upside down and backwards on the ground glass of his 'view camera'. Likewise the

large glass negatives that he printed from were an inversion of the final photograph's positive image, in which light areas appear dark and vice versa.

7. *Auralia*, a love for the golden. See note 5.

8. Dodgson took up photography in 1856 as a young man of twenty-four.

9. E.J. Bellocq (1873–1949) was a photographer who took portraits of streetwalkers in the red-light district (Storyville) of New Orleans, c. 1912. In one, the 'woman of the night' is drawing a butterfly on the wall. Following his death in 1949, Bellocq's glass-plate negatives were found in his desk and were later acquired by Lee Friedlander, a photographer in his own right. Friedlander printed directly from the negatives. The printed photographs came into public view when they were included in the exhibition *E.J. Bellocq: Storyville Portraits* at MoMA in New York in 1970. Friedlander is credited for preserving and promoting them.

10. Those familiar with the history of photography know that the Victorian photographer Julia Margaret Cameron (1815–79) made

kudzu ate the South

Sally Mann
Untitled, 1996

Sally Mann
At Warm Springs, 1991

83

processes. He is obsessed with using recipes from the past to produce his pictures. He makes wet-collodion glass negatives using treacle, malt, raspberry juice, raisin syrup, pine-kernel juice, milk, liquorice juice, chestnut juice, ginger wine, beer, tea, coffee, gum arabic, opium and morphine.[11] He makes positive prints with albumen (the technique that he favours) using eggs, lots of eggs.[12] Egg whites that is. He separates the whites from the yolks and adds them to a salt solution. He then beats them together in a froth. The beating creates a uniform liquid. Although the Reverend insists on fresh eggs, the albumen mixture has to be left to age for a week. He then uses it until he can no longer stand the smell.[13]

The Reverend's darkroom really stinks. When preparing a new batch of albumen, the Reverend sends Nancy directly to her glazed hen house to bring in the most recently laid eggs for a new batch of albumen. (He really prefers duck eggs; they produce the finest prints, but they are harder to come by.[14])

Sometimes the Reverend lets Nancy under the black cloth tent of his large-format camera. Through the lens of his giant camera, Nancy is privy to a world backwards and upside down. When the Reverend brings Nancy into his darkroom, Nancy sees a world where black is white and white is black.[15]

Right now, the Reverend and Nancy are floating down the river in an old wooden rowboat painted green. It is a golden, if stinking, afternoon. The bad smell is not from the Reverend's albumen, but from the stench of things growing and deteriorating in the hot, wet, Virginia air of summer.

The odour goes unnoticed by these two: either because they are true Southerners, who often overlook the smells of the South (like the reek of sulphur in their well water), or because they are floating above the pitfalls of reality. Probably both.

her coalhouse into her darkroom and her glazed hen house into her glass house (photographic studio).

11. The 1850s have been appropriately labelled 'the culinary period of photography' because, during this period, photographers fixed their images with 'sugar, caramel, treacle, malt, raspberry syrup, ginger wine, sherry, beer … vinegar and skimmed milk' (Alison and Helmut Gernsheim, *The History of Photography*, Oxford: Oxford University Press, 1955, p. 258). For an excellent analysis of the concept of the culinary appetite of the photographing eye, see Olivier Richon's 'A Devouring Eye', in *Olivier Richon: Fotografie 1989–2004*, Milan: Silvana Editoriale, 2004, pp. 25–33.

12. Throughout Dodgson's photographic career, he stuck with the wet-collodion process for developing his glass negatives and almost exclusively favoured making his positive prints out of albumen.

13. In *The Photographic Experience, 1839–1914: Images and Attitudes* (University Park, PA: Penn State Press, 1994), Heinz K. Henisch and Bridget Ann Henisch discuss the culinary aspects of early photography, emphasising the strong family ties between chemistry and cooking. They describe the process of making albumen prints, and the resulting stench, as follows: 'To make the albumen mixture, egg whites were separated from the yolks, added to a salt solution, and then beaten to a froth. The beating was necessary to break down the different protein structures and create a uniform liquid. Although much emphasis was put on the importance of using fresh eggs, the albumen mixture itself had to be left to age for a week. After that, it could be stored for some time longer, and used until even the modest dedicated darkroom fanatic began to have misgivings … No wonder that Lydia Bonfils, wife and mother of two famous photographers in Lebanon, was once heard to exclaim, "I never want to smell another egg again," after forty years of valiant whisking' (p. 56). The authors go on to describe the resulting stench of the 'industry' of making albumen paper: 'The albumen process dominated the world of photography from the mid-1850s to the 1890s … creating a great need for reliable commercial sources … [The] German city of Dresden became the capital of the albumen world … In 1888 the Dresdener Albuminfabriken A.G. produced 18,674 reams of albumen paper. To make the coating for each of these reams, twenty-seven dozen egg whites were needed and so, in the course of one year, this factory alone used over six million eggs … As all the factories in the city believed in encouraging the albumen to ferment for several days before it was made into a solution, the atmosphere must have been overwhelming, and it comes as no surprise to learn that Dresden paper could always be identified by the smell alone' (p. 56).

14. In the nineteenth century, some photographers felt that duck eggs produced the finest albumen prints.

15. 'Alice reflected later in life on the pleasure of her involvement with Carroll in his photography. "Much more exciting than being photographed," she recalled, "was being allowed to go into the dark room, and watch him develop the large glass plates. What could be more thrilling than to see the negative gradually take shape … Besides, the dark room was so mysterious, and we felt that any adventures might happen there!' Alice Hargreaves (née Liddell), as quoted in *Lewis Carroll's Alice: The Photographs, Books, Papers and Personal Effects of Alice Liddell and her Family*, New York and London: Sotheby's, 2001, p. 51.

16. As Roger Taylor has written about Dodgson's reverence for children: 'He revered children for their loveliness and grace, sincerely believing that they were pure, innocent beings untouched by the sins and the troubles of the world.

These feelings of reverence are perfectly expressed in the stanza he composed to Alice Murdoch [another child-friend, whom Dodgson photographed in 1856] in which he referred to her as a celestial blessing' (Roger Taylor and Edward Wakeling, *Lewis Carroll: Photographer*, Princeton and Oxford: Princeton University Press, 2002, pp. 56–7).

17. Much has been written about Dodgson's stutter, including his own personal accounts of his speech impediment, which he claimed was 'always worse in reading (when I can see difficult words before they come) than in speaking' (Morton Cohen (ed.), *The Letters of Lewis Carroll*, 2 vols., London: Macmillan, 1979, vol. 2, p. 1154).

Carroll patterned the extinct Dodo who lives in Wonderland after himself, in a play on how he stuttered his own name: Do-do-do-dodgson.

Some commentators have claimed, perhaps rightly and wrongly, that Dodgson lost his stutter in the presence of little girls. Lindsay Smith, in her fine essay 'Lewis Carroll: Stammering, Photography and the Voice of Infancy' (*Journal of Visual Culture* 3.1 [2004]), sums up the curing and not-curing effect of the child's presence on Dodgson as follows: 'there persists in the criticism [regarding Carroll's stammer] a persuasive notion that, in the manner of a stage actor adopting a persona, Carroll enjoyed a reprieve from his stammer in the performative realm of photographing little girls. However since at least one of his young models, May Barber, recalls the occasion of Carroll's stammering as "rather terrifying", we can't accept this reading as definitive. She notes that "it wasn't exactly a stammer, because there was no noise, he just opened his mouth. But there was a wait, a very nervous wait from everybody's point of view: it was very curious" ... There is little doubt that in spite of his stammer ... Carroll felt very comfortable among children. Yet, a belief that Carroll's "hesitation" was cured in the company of little girls mythologizes the nature of that association and fuels a line of argument that promotes his reluctance or inability to mature' (p. 97).

Virginia Woolf, Julia Margaret Cameron's great-niece, speaks of Carroll's reluctance to mature as follows: in him, there was an 'untinted jelly [that] contained within it a perfectly hard crystal. It contained childhood. And this is very strange, for childhood normally fades slowly ... But it was not so with Lewis Carroll ... It lodged in him whole and entire. He could not disperse it. And therefore as he grew older, this impediment in the centre of his being, this hard block of pure childhood, starved the mature man of nourishment' ('Lewis Carroll' [1939], in *Aspects of Alice*, ed. Robert Phillips, London: Victor Gollancz, 1972, pp. 48–9).

18. Kudzu is the fast growing 'mile-a-minute vine', which is often referred to as the 'vine that ate the South'. It was introduced to the US from Japan in 1876 and is now out of control. Few people appreciate it, but the American photographer Sally Mann, also from Virginia, does. Mann, who is famed for her series of sensual photographs of her own children taken in the 1980s (which are often compared to Dodgson's pictures), has taken remarkable images of kudzu, as part of her more recent landscape series. Like Dodgson, she has used a large-format camera and the wet-collodion process to develop magical images of the vine eating up Virginia and Georgia. See Sally Mann, *Mother Land*, New York, Boston, London: Bullfinch Press, 2005, p. 9 and p. 37. For comparisons between Dodgson's photographs of children and those by Sally Mann, see Carol Mavor, *Pleasures Taken: Performances of Sexuality and Loss in Victorian Photographs*, Durham and London: Duke University Press, 1995; and Carol Mavor, *Becoming: The Photographs of Clementina, Viscountess Hawarden*, Durham and London: Duke University Press, 1995. For the relationship between Mann's photographs of the landscape and of her children, see Carol Mavor, '"Phantoms of the Past, Dear Companions of Childhood,

The air, soaked with the rain of big everyday thunderstorms, is so thick, so viscous that you can see it, catch it, like lightning bugs in a glass jar at night.

The trees are growing as thick as the treacle-brown water they are floating on.

Seven-year-old Nancy is listening to the Reverend's fairy story drone on. She has brought along her doll. She keeps it in an old wire birdcage. The Reverend is but thirty-two, but he has the strained, quivery voice of a man of sixty-two. He is staring at her; really staring.

He quivers: 'N-n-n-na-na-nan, ya-ya-ya yerr a celestial b-b-b-blessing.'[16]

With a Southern girl's accent, heavy with the syrupy drawl of her mother and grandmother, Nancy hollers: 'Sto-op lookin at me-ay!' And then, she slowly tosses the Reverend a splash of tepid, soupy river water. It leaves a stain of silt on his started-out-clean-and-white-this-morning-short-sleeved-button-down-collar-50-50 poly-cotton shirt, which was already damp with sweat.

'N-n-n-na-na-nan, I am not st-t-t-t-aring,' stutters the lying Reverend. He calls her Nan or sometimes just 'N', because both are easier to say than the full 'Nancy', without stuttering. (The Reverend does not really lose his stutter in the presence of little girls, as many claim. In fact, little girls make the stutter worse.[17])

The air is soaked with the sound of living things. Nancy can hear the sound of the strangling kudzu vines growing. Kudzu is enchanting and terrifying, cousin to the beanstalk that grew from Jack's magic beans, known to grow a foot a night.[18]

Not long ago, Nancy's doll (a birthday gift from the Reverend) had begun to grow like kudzu. She had fallen in love with the doll at first sight. Like a photograph, her doll was infuriatingly divine in its silence. On the night of her birthday

Nancy brought the doll to bed with her. Later that night, she suddenly woke up from an exhausting dream. Drenched with sweat, she saw that her doll had been growing with the magic of kudzu. As a precaution, Nancy put her beloved doll in a wire birdcage.[19] The doll's growth has since been arrested. The doll is now forever little, as if she were caught in a photograph. Nancy is no longer afraid of her doll, but she is afraid of these trees wearing aprons, shirts, pants and tall hats of kudzu. They are cousins to the strangling trees of Oz. The Reverend once read *The Wizard of Oz* to Nancy, in this very boat.

Nancy is afraid of the sound of soft, furry, black Virginia spiders the size of hummingbirds.

Nancy is afraid of the slithery sound of long snakes.

Nancy is not afraid of the no-sound of slow turtles.

Nancy is not afraid of the cushiony sound of rubbery, saucer-sized mushrooms, which grow overnight in response to the summer's everyday thunderstorms.

Nancy is drawn to the sound of the 'Who cooks for you? Who cooks for you all?' hoot of the owl.

And then, under the hot gaze of the Reverend (who is still staring, despite claims otherwise), with her nose full of pong, her ears full of the forest and river sounds, Nancy begins to feel very sleepy and slow. Somewhere between not being awake and not being asleep, she sees a Rabbit. He is naked like rabbits often are.[20] 'Nothing so *very* remarkable in that,'[21] thought Nancy to herself. He is standing in the dark corner of a dilapidated brick house; his body is that of a lean, muscular, young man. His face is white. She is curious to know if he has red eyes. Here in this hot, wet, woodsy place, life is remarkably still. But Nancy is beginning to move, if slowly, like molasses. Nancy is easing her way

Vanished Friends": Making Sense of Sally Mann's Trees', in Lorna Collins and Elizabeth Rush (eds.), *Making Sense*, New York and Berne: Peter Lang, forthcoming 2011–12.

19. Dodgson often posed his child-friends like dolls in costumes of fancy dress. On occasion he also photographed his girl-models with dolls. In an 1864 photograph, Agnes Price holds a doll face to face, seemingly mocking the proper, nurturing mother. She is a double of Alice holding the baby-turned-pig. As Nina Auerbach writes (*Romantic Imprisonment: Women and other Glorified Outcasts*, New York: Columbia University Press, 1986, p. 167): 'the doll becomes less a thing to nourish than a thing to eat'.

20. The Rabbit of this fairy tale is inspired by the American photographer Francesca Woodman (1958–81) and her photograph of a man wearing a rabbit mask (*Untitled*, Boulder, Colorado 1972–75), taken when the artist was still an adolescent. Woodman's surrealist approach feels inspired by Lewis Carroll's writing and Dodgson's photographs. As the Irish critic and novelist Brian Dillon has written in a review of an exhibition of Woodman's work at London's Victoria Miro gallery (*London Review of Books*, vol. 33, no. 2, 20 January 2011): 'The atmosphere in her photographs is literary – tricked up out of Lewis Carroll, Poe and Surrealism – as well as knowingly indebted to photographers from Julia Margaret Cameron to Duane Michals'.

Beyond the wide historical time difference is the fact that Woodman is a 'girl' who began photography as a child, aged thirteen, whose body of work is almost entirely self-portraits. But as with Dodgson, so in Woodman – who often wore black Chinese-style Mary Jane shoes (sometimes even in her nude self-portraits), flaunted her long blonde hair and had a high feminine voice – there seems to have been that 'untinted jelly [that] contained within it a perfectly hard crystal ... of childhood' (see note 17). As Woodman once commented to a friend and fellow artist in regard to her own slightly Alicious look: 'You have to admit there's something questionable about women who have long blonde hair to their waist past the age of seventeen'. Or as the barely adult Woodman wrote in her journal, in 1975, in regard to menacing romance and a 'sideways slide of eyes': 'This is icky. I so much preferred being a child.' See Chris Townsend, *Francesca Woodman: Scattered in Space and Time*, exh. cat., London: Phaidon, 2006, pp. 247 and 243.

21. At the start of *Alice's Adventures in Wonderland*, when Alice first sees the White Rabbit, Carroll writes: 'There was nothing so *very* remarkable in that; nor did Alice think it so *very* much out of the way to hear the Rabbit say to itself "Oh dear! Oh dear! I shall be too late!" (when she thought it over afterwards, it occurred to her that she ought to have wondered at this, but at the time it all seemed quite natural)' (*The Annotated Alice*, pp. 11–12).

22. When Alice is falling down the rabbit hole, Carroll writes, seemingly in reference to Eve and the Fall of Man in Genesis: 'Down, down, down. Would the fall never come to an end?' (*The Annotated Alice*, p. 13). And like Eve, Alice is a sign of eating, consumption and impending sexuality. When Alice eats, it changes her size, suggesting a woman's developing and changing body, from the sporting of hips and breasts to the swelling pregnant belly (which might look like a serpent that has swallowed its prey).

23. All of the photographs described refer to actual photographs by Dodgson. One of these is Dodgson's nude *Portrait of Evelyn Hatch* c. 1878. Dodgson's first reference to photographing a nude child is in a diary entry dated 21 May 1867: 'Mrs. L. brought Beatrice, and I took a photograph of the two; and several of Beatrice alone, "Sans habilement [sic]"'; Helmut Gernsheim, *Lewis Carroll, Photographer*, New York: Dover, 1969, p. 65. Agnes Grace Weld posed as Little Red Riding Hood, looking more like the wolf, ready to eat the viewer up (1857). Irene MacDonald, daughter of the famed Victorian fairy-tale writer George MacDonald, posed as a partly undressed odalisque amidst fur and Oriental rugs, with her Mary Janes peeking through (1863). Alexandra Kitchin posed for Dodgson dressed variously as a Chinaman, a Turk, a princess, and in a tableau of St George and the dragon. Dodgson called her Xie for short or even just 'X', which may have been easier for the stammering Dodgson to say. See Carol Mavor, 'Mouthing Metonymy in Lewis Carroll: Alice's Alicious Appetite', in Dennis Denisoff (ed.), *Victorian Children and Consumerism*, London: Ashgate, 2008, p. 105.

out of the boat and into the caramel-coloured river water to swim to shore, in pursuit of the Rabbit. While swimming towards the river's edge, she feels mysterious, as if she is swimming in her own tears.

As soon as she reaches the Rabbit's house, he runs inside. Nancy opens the door, without knocking, and runs after the Rabbit. She seems to have forgotten her manners. Once inside the house, she is just in time to see him open the cellar door and run down the steps. She takes off after him.

Down, down, down, would the steps never end?[22]

Step after step, Nancy becomes increasingly tired and begins to move more and more slowly. The air is turning cooler and cooler. She stops to catch her breath. She notices that the stairwell is filled with cupboards and bookshelves. Here and there, Nancy sees photographs of children, many in costume: as Chinamen and Turks, as St George and the Dragon, as Little Riding Hood, as beggars and more. Some are resting or asleep. One girl is splayed out on a couch. Another girl is a partly undressed odalisque amidst fur and Oriental rugs, with her Mary Janes peeking through. There are more pictures of girls than boys. One girl has no clothes on at all.[23]

What Nancy cannot see is that she is walking through a museum of love.

Finally, in the coolness of the deep, deep cellar, Nancy finds herself looking into a long passage full of closed doors. The Rabbit is just in sight. Away goes Nancy, like the wind, after the Rabbit. Just as she hears him say, 'Oh my ears and whiskers, how late it is getting!' he vanishes. Where could he have gone? Perhaps behind a door? Nancy discovers that all the doors are locked. But three have peepholes.

The first peephole reveals a combined bedroom and photography laboratory. There is a small, unmade bed. The walls are lined with books. There are bottles carefully labelled: treacle, malt, raspberry juice, raisin syrup, pine-kernel juice, milk, liquorice juice, chestnut juice, ginger wine, beer, tea, coffee, gum arabic, opium and morphine. There are pewter trays, an ordinary light bulb covered with red paper, a pair of white gloves and a pile of glass negatives. Nancy recognises this room at once, as the Reverend's own laboratory-bedroom. But how could that be? There is a slight odour of ether, eggs, gold cyanide and ginger wine.

The second peephole reveals a beautiful, small, brown rabbit lying on its side, on a patch of green grass. The rabbit is asleep (or dead).[24] His tender, furry white belly is the picture of innocence. Through the round hole, Nancy sees a young woman's hands gently drawing the front paws of the rabbit towards its hind legs, as if it were preparing for a leap. Then, the young woman's hands carefully pull the front paws and the hind legs away from each other, as if the rabbit were soaring through the air. The animating movement is repeated over and over: each time a bit faster than the time before. The scene has a Muybridge touch.[25] Nancy can just barely hear the girl breathily saying over again and again: 'run rabbit, run rabbit, run, run, run'.[26] There is a slight odour of grass, rabbit and whiskers.

The third peephole reveals a young girl on a theatrical stage speaking to Humpty Dumpty.[27] Nancy cannot hear what the girl is saying. There is no audience, save for Nancy peering in. The giant egg makes Nancy think of all of the albumen that the Reverend could make out of him and how much *crème renversée au caramel* her mother could make out of him. There is a slight odour of starched and ironed cotton apron, Mary Janes and puffed sleeves.

Looking through the peepholes is like looking through the Reverend's telescope, at the end of which he has glued a tiny picture of Nancy.[28] When the Reverend looks through it, you can

24. The rabbit here is 'speaking' to the condition of photography. Almost all photographs of people, even animals, suggest the contradictory doubleness of the photograph's indexical nature: an evasion of time (like an everlasting fairy-tale), and a record of the death of a moment (forever gone). Images by Dodgson (and Cameron) of children who appear to be asleep are not far from the Victorian postmortem photographs of children, dressed in their most precious clothes, holding a favoured toy, framed by beautiful flowers and silken pillows. Such photographs reveal death as a contradiction inherent to the life of the medium itself.

25. Eadward Muybridge (1830–1904) was one of the great pioneers in photography, famous for his filmic images of animals in motion.

26. This scene is inspired by Samantha Sweeting's 2007 *Run rabbit, run rabbit, run, run, run*. There is a touch of Alice and the 'grim' fairy-tale threaded through much of Sweeting's oeuvre. Particularly *Wonderlandish* is Sweeting's 2009 photograph *In came the lamb*, in which the artist nurses a lamb in the sprit of Alice with her baby-turned-pig: 'As soon as she had made out the proper way of nursing it (which was to twist it up in a sort of knot, and then keep tight hold of its right ear and left foot, so as to prevent its undoing itself), she carried it out into the open air. "If I don't take this child away with me," thought Alice, "they're sure to kill it in a day or two. Wouldn't it be murder to leave it behind?"' (*The Annotated Alice*, p. 63).

27. This scene is inspired by the photograph of Bambi Linn as Alice for the American Repertory Theater's 1947 staging of *Alice in Wonderland*, which appeared on the cover of *Life* magazine. Alice is shown listening to Humpty Dumpy, the unstammering, yet foolish, self-professed Master of Language. As the giant anthropomorphic egg tells Alice: 'When I use a word … it means just what I choose it to mean – neither more nor less' (*Through the Looking-glass*, in *The Annotated Alice*, p. 213).

28. I have written elsewhere about the fact that Dodgson glued a small photograph of Alice Liddell inside the end of his telescope: 'one gaze and the world would stop still, every star would be Alicious' (*Pleasures Taken*, p. 33).

29. This is from the terminal acrostic poem to *Through the Looking-glass*, which spells out 'ALICE PLEASANCE LIDDELL', while recalling the 4th of July boat trip up the Thames when Dodgson first told Alice the original story (*The Annotated Alice*, p. 273).

30. This scene is inspired by Francesca Woodman's photograph of a hand resting on top of a mushroom-like stool, holding a small white child's glove (*Untitled*, New York 1979–80). Woodman must have been thinking of Alice. Dodgson himself was very fond of gloves. He was teased as a boy at school for wearing gloves at unexpected times and continued this eccentricity into adulthood. As Martin Gardner has noted: 'Gloves were as important to Carroll as they were to the Rabbit … "He was a little eccentric in his clothes," Isa Bowman writes in *The Story of Lewis Carroll* (J.M. Dent, 1899). "In the coldest weather he would never wear an overcoat, and had a curious habit of always wearing, in all seasons of the year, a pair of grey and black cotton gloves"' (*The Annotated Alice*, p. 40, n. 6). In the early days, photography was called 'the black art': the collodion (which contained silver nitrate) would stain your fingers with evidence of what you had been up to, perhaps a link to Dodgson's own obsession with gloves and his White Rabbit who wears them.

31. In a letter to Isa Bowman's sister Maggie, Dodgson tells a hilarious linguistic tale of kittens who are made to wear gloves on all four paws unless they are catching a mouse. The moment that they have caught the mouse, they must 'pop their gloves on again, because they know we can't love them without their gloves. For, you see "gloves" have got "love" *inside* them – there's none *outside*' (*The Annotated Alice*, pp. 40–1, n. 6).

The giant egg makes Nancy think of all of the albumen
that the Reverend could make out of him
and how much Crème renversée au caramel
that her mother could make out of him.

left: American Repertory Theatre stage production
Alice in Wonderland, 1947

hear him softly singing a song: 'Still she haunts me, phantomwise, / Nancy moving under skies / Never seen by waking eyes… Lingering in the golden gleam – / Life, what is it but a dream?'[29]

Suddenly, Nancy comes upon an old, round stool with a white padded top, which has the queer appearance of a toadstool. It has come out of nowhere, like mushrooms in a Virginia forest, after a summer rain. Upon the stool sits a tiny golden key. Nancy immediately tries the key in all of the doors. Either the locks are too large or the key is too small. She tries all the locks again, just to make sure, and, in doing so, she comes to a low curtain, which she had not seen before. Behind the little violet velvet curtain is a green door. It is only eighteen inches high. She tries the key and it fits. Looking through the open door, Nancy sees the loveliest garden. In the far distance is a little house, much like the Reverend's own. But Nancy cannot even get her head through the doorway. If only she could shut up like a telescope.

There seems to be no use in waiting by the little door, so she returns to the mushroom stool, half hoping she might find another key on it, or at any rate a book of rules for shutting people up like telescopes. This time she finds a little white glove on the stool, like one the Reverend would wear for handling glass negatives, only smaller.[30] The Reverend once told her that he can only love with 'gloves': for you see 'gloves' have 'love' inside them.[31]

The glove is, in fact, even a bit snug for Nancy; but she forces her hand into it anyways, just to see how it would feel. 'What a curious feeling!' says Nancy. 'I must be shutting up like a telescope!'

Nancy is now fourteen inches tall, an ideal size for going through the little door into that lovely garden and on to the house. Once through the door, she follows a long and winding path to the little house. The flowers along the way are

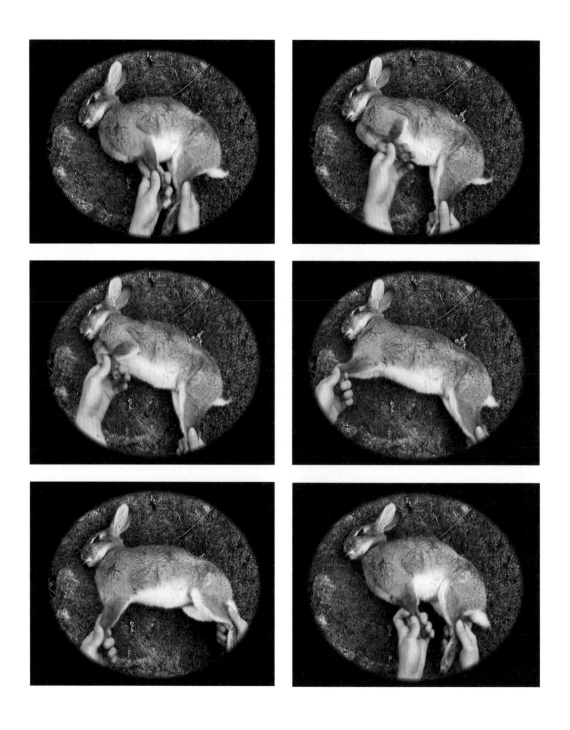

the scene has a Muybridge touch

Samantha Sweeting
Stills from the video *Run rabbit, run rabbit, run, run, run,* 2007

He is naked like rabbits often are.
There is nothing so very remarkable in that.

Francesca Woodman
Untitled, 1972-75

charming: white daisies with yellow centres. She thinks she hears them talking to her, but she carries on.[32] Finally she arrives: over the door is a sign, with gold letters that reads 'M. RABBIT'. She knocks on the door. It opens. The Rabbit appears, naked as before: nothing unusual in that. The Rabbit smiles flatly at her and gives her his paw. She shakes his too-adorable paw (with her ungloved hand). Her mind flashes back to the paws of the little brown rabbit: she hopes that he is off and running now.

The Rabbit, as he stands tall before her, is indifferent to her. Or is he hiding something from her? He seems to know her, even love her, from another world.

'You from here?' Nancy asks the Rabbit.

Without answering, the Rabbit notices her other hand and says in a rather monotonous voice, 'Why have you stolen my other glove?' Nancy was sure she had not. Nevertheless, she hands over the glove to the Rabbit. She wonders how it will fit his too-adorable paw. 'I am about ready to print some photographs and I am all out of eggs. Mary Ann, fetch me some eggs this instant!' 'Why,' thinks Nancy, 'he has taken me for his maid!'[33] Nancy is offended, but she is curious to see his pictures. So, she goes off looking for chickens, or preferably ducks, in hopes that they have laid some eggs.

The first thing she discovers is a real mushroom. It is huge. But perhaps not as huge as you might think, given that Nancy is now only fourteen inches tall.

She stretches herself up onto tiptoe, and peeps over the edge of the mushroom. Her eyes immediately meet those of a large blue caterpillar.

'Who are *you* and what do *you* want?' asks the Caterpillar.

'I am Nancy and I am after fresh eggs.'

32. The white flowers with their yellow centres are a doubling of the eggs which began this story, and allude to the talking daisies in Chapter 2 of *Through the Looking-glass*, 'The Garden of Live Flowers'. Alice threatens the daisies to silence by telling them that she will pick them if they do not hold their tongues.

33. In *Alice's Adventures in Wonderland*, the White Rabbit also calls Alice 'Mary Ann', indicating – to Alice's chagrin – that he has mistaken her for a housemaid. At the time, Mary Ann was a 'euphemism' for 'servant girl'. Of interest is the fact that Julia Margaret Cameron actually had a housemaid named Mary Anne (see *The Annotated Alice*, p. 38, n. 2.) Likewise, earlier in *Wonderland*, Alice fears that she has become 'Mabel', a girl without means and who knows so 'very little!' Distressed, her eyes filled with tears, Alice exclaims 'I must be Mabel after all, and I shall have to go and live in that poky little house, and have next to no toys to play with, and oh, ever so many lessons to learn!' (*The Annotated Alice*, pp. 23–4).

Dodgson's own class anxiety undoubtedly fed Alice's. While the photographer enjoyed dressing Alice Liddell up as a beggar with her hand opened for change, as in his c. 1858 image of her, Dodgson preferred his models to be of the proper class. As Dodgson wrote to a grown Beatrice Hatch, regarding a 'sweet-looking' twelve-year-old from the wrong side of the tracks: 'Some of my little *actress*-friends are of a *rather* lower status than myself. But, below a certain line, it is hardly wise to let a girl have a "gentleman" friend – even one of 62!' For more on this letter and Dodgson's reluctance to befriend and photograph children of the working class, see Mavor, *Pleasures Taken*, pp. 35–42.

She offers the Reverend two perfect eggs
and he is taken with how serpentine this just-right
girl looks.
She looks and she feels good enough to eat.

Emmet Gowin
Nancy, Danville, Virginia, 1969

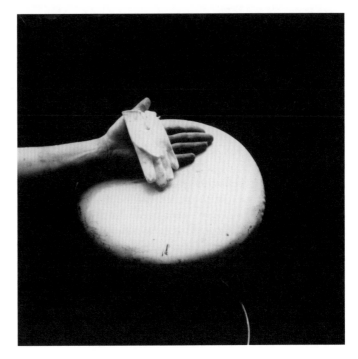

The glove was, in fact, even a bit snug for Nancy,
but she forces her hand into it anyways, just to see
how it would feel.

Francesca Woodman
Untitled, 1979-80

'What kind of eggs?' asks the Caterpillar. 'I hope you are not after caterpillar eggs,' he adds.

'Of course not,' replies Nancy. 'They're too small.'

'They're not,' the Caterpillar rebukes her. 'Well, they are if you want to make albumen photographs.' 'How about the eggs of a pigeon?' the Caterpillar suggests.

Nancy is excited at this prospect. Perhaps pigeon eggs might provide the Rabbit's photographs with a glorious sheen and exquisite detail, even beyond that of duck albumen.

'Where can I find a pigeon's nest?' enquires Nancy.

'Why, up there,' replies the Caterpillar, turning his slow cumbersome head skywards, looking up with his unusually large, bespectacled eyes. Nancy had not noticed his glasses until now. (She had once read that caterpillars have very poor eyesight.) Nancy looks up and all she can see are the verdant leaves and the branches of some huge trees.

'How can I ever get all the way up there?' queries Nancy.

'Why, by eating a bit of the left side of the mushroom,' says the strange Caterpillar as he slithers off the mushroom and goes away.

'And now which is right and which is left?' Nancy asks herself, her arms stretched around the huge mushroom top. Playing it safe, she decides to put some chunks of the mushroom from what she thinks might be the left-hand side in her left pocket and some chunks of what she thinks might be the right-hand side in her right pocket. She nibbles a bit of (what might be) the right-side piece to try out its effect. In a flash, her chin nearly hits her shoes. But before hitting bottom, she manages to swallow a morsel from

34. Many writers have taken pleasure in the homonyms of 'little' and Alice 'Liddell', which must have amused Carroll, who made great use of punning in all of his writing.

35. Alice's appetite in Wonderland is suggestive of the adolescent growth that lies before her. This appetite, ranging from the voracious to the delicate, is signalled with the turn of nearly every *Wonderland* page: from being accused of eating eggs by the Pigeon, to her disappointment in finding the orange marmalade jar empty, to quickly finishing off a drink that boasts 'a sort of mixed flavour of cherry-tart, custard, pineapple, roast turkey, toffy and hot buttered toast' (*The Annotated Alice*, p. 17), to passing out comfits as prizes, to eating a cake with currants that spell out EAT ME, to eating cakes transformed out of pebbles, to swallowing bits of mushroom, to imagining whether cats eat bats or bats eat cats, to talking about cats who eat mice and dogs who eat rats. Alice's eclectic tastes suggest impurity and indignity, considered by the Pigeon as equivalent to eating one's unhatched offspring, nothing short of cannibalism. As the Pigeon says to Alice: 'You're looking for eggs, I know *that* well enough; and what does it matter to me whether you're a girl or a serpent?' (*The Annotated Alice*, p. 17).
   The coupling of sensual sexuality with eating is evident in Dodgson's 1860 photograph of Edith, Lorina and Alice Liddell, entitled *Open Your Mouth and Shut Your Eyes*. In the photograph, Lorina is dropping a cherry into Alice's mouth, as she stands before her with her eyes closed.
   Dodgson here is nibbling on what Maria Tatar has named 'folkloric cannibalism', as is found in the Grimms' *Hansel and Gretel* and *The Juniper Tree* or Perrault's Tom Thumb (Maria Tatar, *Off with their Heads! Fairy Tales and the Culture of Childhood*, Princeton: Princeton University Press, 1992, p. 194). Likewise, '[e]ating and being eaten inspires one of the most common games adults play with babies' and children (Marina Warner, *No Go the Bogeyman: Scaring, Lulling and Making Mock*, New York: Farrar, Straus and Giroux, 1998, p. 139).

36. In *Wonderland*, Alice exclaims to the Caterpillar: 'three inches is such a wretched height to be'. The Caterpillar angrily disagrees, for it is 'exactly three inches high' (*The Annotated Alice*, p. 53).

her left pocket and immediately experiences a soaring effect.

'It works,' claims Nancy, not so much surprised as satisfied. Nancy is now high up in the trees. She is eighty feet and three and one-half inches tall. Her neck is stretched far, far away from her feet. Her nose can touch the blue sky. And there, right under her sky-high nose, at the top of a very leafy tree, is a pigeon's nest, full of eggs.

'Serpent!' screams the angry Pigeon, soaring towards her out of nowhere.

'I'm *not*!' says Nancy indignantly. 'I'm a little girl,'[34] she adds, this time in a more friendly, polite tone.

'You're a serpent,' says the Pigeon, now full of extra contempt. 'With such a neck as that, I can see you are a serpent. Furthermore, I saw you greedily eyeing my eggs.'[35]

Nancy starts to say that she would never eat the Pigeon's eggs (at last not raw), but she realises that she is facing a losing battle. There is nothing to do but simply steal the Pigeon's eggs. And so she does.

The Pigeon screams 'CANNIBAL!', as she flies in close enough to meet Nancy eye to eye. Just as Nancy recalls how in the story of Cinderella the pigeons peck out both eyes of the wicked false sisters, the eighty-feet-and-three-and-one-half-inches-tall, seven-year-old girl remembers that there is a bit of right-sided mushroom in her right-hand pocket. And all at once, Nancy quickly swallows a morsel of right-sided mushroom. Within a second, Nancy is back to being fourteen inches high. Not such a wretched height[36] after all; rather pleasant, in fact.

It is not long before Nancy is back under the sign with gold letters that reads 'M. RABBIT'. Feeling rather at ease about her friendship with the Rabbit, she lets herself in without knocking.

She finds her way towards the darkroom, following its smell of ether, eggs, gold cyanide and ginger wine. She opens the darkroom door and it is in fact dark, save for the light that she has just let in. She sees that the Rabbit's eyes are red; for he is using his red eyes like 'safelights' to illuminate his darkroom for developing his negatives. For a flash, she sees the magic of the pictures developing. But the inverted images disappear quickly with the light, like dream rushes, and she suddenly finds herself back on the rowboat.

The Reverend is droning on. He is staring at her, really staring.

'Way-ache up, Nancy dahr-er!' the Reverend is saying. 'Whaa-eye, what a long slee-eep you've ha-ad! I was fixin to pought wah-tahh on yer face.'

All the while, the Reverend is thinking that he must photograph Nancy again, as quickly as possible, while she is still so little, so as to remember her child-life as his.[37]

The next morning, Nancy comes by to see the Reverend at his house. She offers the Reverend two perfect eggs and he is taken with how serpentine this just-right girl looks. She looks and she feels good enough to eat.[38]

THE END

37. This passage and the one in the darkroom allude to the moment in *Through the Looking-glass* when Alice is in the boat with the Sheep and is leaning over to pick dream flora: the 'ends of [her] tangled hair [are] dipping into the water', as she gathers 'one bunch after another of the darling scented rushes'. Frustrated at not being able to reach the most attractive flowers, Alice exclaims: 'The prettiest are always further!' As she begins to 'arrange her new-found treasures', she sees 'that the rushes had begun to fade, and to lose all their scent and beauty from the very moment she picked them' (*The Annotated Alice*, p. 204). As Gardner remarks: 'it is possible that Carroll thought of these dream-rushes as symbols of his child-friends. The loveliest seem to be the most distant, just out of reach, and once picked, they quickly fade and lose their scent and beauty' (*The Annotated Alice*, p. 204, n. 16). Of course to photograph little girls is a way to pick them without compromising their beauty. By preserving his child-friends with wet-collodion and albumen, like *Looking-glass* insects, Dodgson could believe in the fantasy that their youth would never fade.

38. According to Adam Phillips, kissing is 'aim-inhibited eating'. Likewise, Phillips contends, 'when we kiss we devour the object by caressing it; we eat it, in a sense, but sustain its presence' (*On Kissing, Tickling and Being Bored*, Cambridge, MA: Harvard University Press, 1994, p. 97). It is in this way that a photograph can be read as a kiss, as 'aim-inhibited eating': it consumes while leaving the integrity of the subject unmarked. A great portrait, like Gowin's of Nancy with her eggs, could be described as like a kiss; for it, too, 'blurs the distinction between giving and taking' (Phillips, *On Kissing*, p. 97). In Gowin's picture, the 'author' of the image is undecidable. As Gowin has remarked on *Nancy* (in an interview with Sally Gall, *Bomb* 58, Winter 1997): 'If I thought anything was original in my work, it was accepting the here and now, and then letting it show me what was important. The little child crossing her arms and showing me those two eggs. She just came to me with two eggs and crossed her arms. And I thought, that is the wisdom of the body. To whatever extent that she knows it, it's her body informing her. It's the same kind of intuition that I wanted to work out of. If she could invent that much, the thing that I could do is be open to the invention. And that is, in essence, just how it happened.' Inspired by photography, the fairy-tale, Lewis Carroll/Charles Dodgson, Emmet Gowin and Alice/Nancy, mine is a story of loving (inhibited and preserving) with the mouth.

98   Paul Nash
Landscape from a Dream, 1936-38

Dorothea Tanning
Eine Kleine Nachtmusik, 1943

Dorothea Tanning
Pincushion to Serve as Fetish, 1965

John Armstrong
Dreaming Head, 1938

Sir Roland Penrose
Le Grand Jour, 1938

F.E. McWilliam
Eye, Nose and Cheek, 1939

Humphrey Jennings
The House in the Woods, 1939-44

right: Conroy Maddox
The Strange Country, 1940

Oskar Kokoschka
Anschluss - Alice im Wunderland, 1941

Max Ernst
Alice in 1941, 1941

left: Max Ernst
Alice in 1939, 1939

Max Ernst
Thirty-three Little Girls Set out for the
White Butterfly Hunt, 1958

right: Max Ernst
Pour les amis d'Alice, 1957

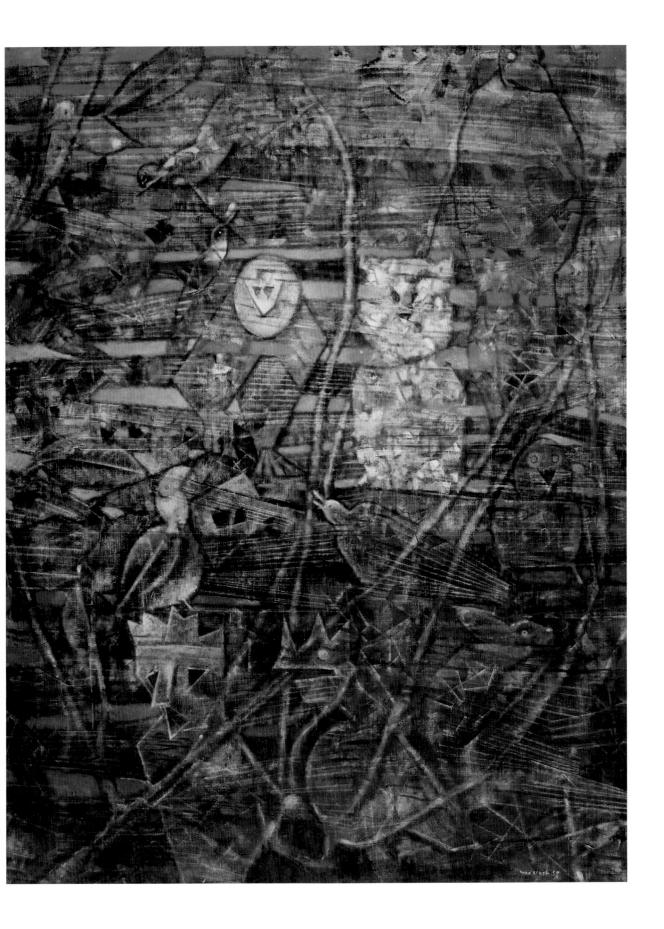

Max Ernst
Alice in Wonderland from *Lewis Carroll's Wunderhorn*, 1970

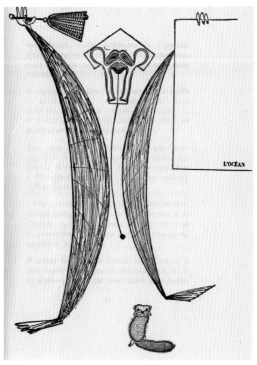

left: Max Ernst
La Chasse au Snark, 1950

right: Max Ernst
The King playing with the Queen, 1954

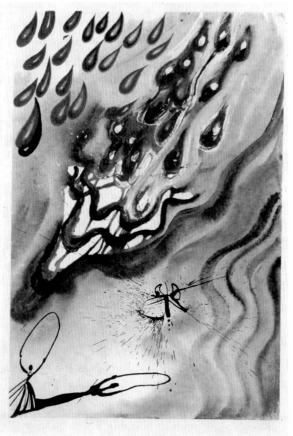

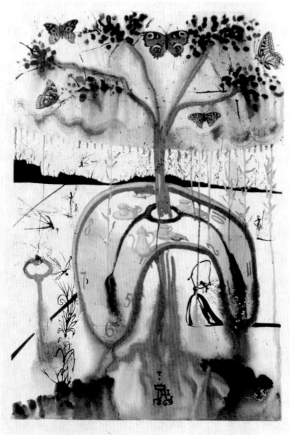

top left: Salvador Dalí
Alice in Wonderland Illustration 5:
Advice from a Caterpiller, 1969

top right: Salvador Dalí
Alice in Wonderland Illustration 2:
The Pool of Tears, 1969

right: Salvador Dalí
Alice in Wonderland Illustration 7:
A Mad Tea Party, 1969

far right: Salvador Dalí
Alice in Wonderland Illustration 4:
The Rabbit sends in a Little Bill, 1969

116

© Disney

Salvador Dalí and Walt Disney
Three film stills from *Destino*, 1946
(completed 2003)

© Disney

© Disney

GILLIAN BEER

TIME'S MANIFOLDS:

– THE –

Alice Books

1. Lewis Carroll, *The Rectory Umbrella* and *Mischmasch*, New York, 1971, pp. 31-32

2. Lewis Carroll, *Alice's Adventures in Wonderland and Through the Looking-Glass and What Alice Found There*, The Centenary Edition, ed. Hugh Haughton, London, 1998, p. 10. Subsequent references are to this edition.

Time and its troubling haunts both the *Alice* books. The young Lewis Carroll was already fascinated by time's quandaries long before writing the *Alice* books. He presented two time puzzles in *The Rectory Umbrella*, the domestic magazine he edited as a boy. Where, he asked, does the day begin and end and Tuesday turn into Wednesday: 'Where, in its passage round the earth, does the day change its name? where does it lose its identity?' He suggests that if we followed the sun round the planet we would find it hard to fix boundaries to the day: 'there would be no distinction at all between each successive day … so that we should have to say, "The Battle of Waterloo happened to-day, about two million hours ago"'.[1] His quirky and ingenious mindset challenges all easy assumptions and, indeed, here presents a puzzle now besetting air travellers and worldwide markets. In his second puzzle he persuades us to prefer the accuracy of a clock that doesn't go at all to one that loses a minute a day. In these early puzzles the Hatter's tea-party is already on its way – and with it all the puzzles about identity and time in the *Alice* books.

Lewis Carroll was also Charles Dodgson, mathematician and logician, and so he was aware of the disturbing arguments that in the mid-nineteenth century newly suggested that our view of space and time within the Euclidean order was local, not universal. As Dodgson, Lewis Carroll was a devout Euclidean. As Lewis Carroll, Dodgson stepped across those boundaries. Alice herself is confident in her occasional role as instructive adult as well as that of enquiring child. She does not observe the time-boundaries marked (by adults) between adult experience and childhood innocence. She wants to know and she wants to dispose. Thresholds may daunt her but she crosses them.

Problems of temporality are fundamental both to logic and to possible worlds. *Wonderland* is preceded by Tenniel's picture of the dapper White Rabbit earnestly consulting his watch. It's the *watch* that startles Alice. A rabbit with pink eyes runs past her.

> There was nothing so *very* remarkable in that; nor did Alice think it so *very* much out of the way to hear the Rabbit say to itself 'Oh dear! Oh dear! I shall be too late!' … but when the Rabbit actually *took a watch out of its waistcoat pocket* [Carroll's italics], and looked at it, and then hurried on, Alice started to her feet, for it flashed across her mind that she had never before seen a rabbit with either a waistcoat-pocket, or a watch to take out of it, and, burning with curiosity, she ran across the field after it.[2]

Belatedness, anxiety, physical props like the watch, all bespeak the individual under the cosh of time-regulated society. This is an animal that speaks, but that's not what the child finds remarkable: it's the accoutrements of adult business, busy-ness. The watch usually signifies the particularly human capacity to invent complex technology. But here we encounter one rabbit who has a watch and can read it, and that sets off the whole sequence of Alice's adventures.

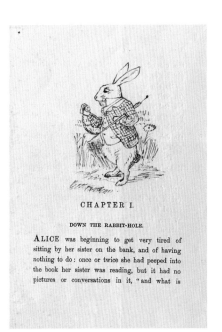

CHAPTER I.

DOWN THE RABBIT-HOLE.

ALICE was beginning to get very tired of sitting by her sister on the bank, and of having nothing to do: once or twice she had peeped into the book her sister was reading, but it had no pictures or conversations in it, "and what is

Watches were established already as the token of human respectability by the time Lewis Carroll was writing *Alice*.[3] Along with the factory clock, watches were the instruments that controlled industrialised labour. There were several new technologies of regularised time in the early nineteenth century and during the period of Lewis Carroll's life and writing. Carroll was a railway enthusiast and the *Alice* books (1865, 1872) appeared in the period when railways and their time-tables had newly required the regularising of time across the whole of the country.[4] Dan Falk quotes an explanatory note from the Great Western Railway timetable in 1841 that sounds a bit like a passage from *Alice* itself:

> London time is kept at all stations on the railway, which is about 4 minutes earlier than Reading time; 5 and a half minutes before Stevenson [*sic*] time; 7 and a half minutes before Cirencester time; 8 minutes before Chippenham time; and 14 minutes before Bridgewater time.[5]

One of Lewis Carroll's own earliest extended inventions, composed around 1850, was a comic operetta for marionette theatre, 'La Guida di Bragia'. Bradshaw's Guide was the bible of all train timetables. The personified Guide has in this play secretly changed all the train times so that the characters have been left in the lurch, too late for departed trains.

Space and time were during Carroll's lifetime coming to be understood more and more as being in intricate and shifting relations. Chronometers kept time at sea and helped in the mapping of colonial claims, bringing time and space together. The new technology of the photograph, of which Lewis Carroll was an early adept, froze and made portable a moment and a place; it also demanded long and rigid passivity from its subjects.[6] And, as Jimena Canales has recently pointed out, a tenth of a second was a newly significant time-unit, particularly in measuring the speed of the nervous system and reaction time.[7]

As so often, Hermann von Helmholtz was in the van of such new discoveries, from the 1850s onwards, working particularly on reaction time.[8] In an *Academy* article in 1870 he summarised many of the non-Euclidean insights that had been gathering during the 1850s and 1860s, most powerfully expressed in Britain by Clifford and Cayley. Helmholtz ended this essay on 'The Axioms of Geometry' by citing what he called Riemann's 'somewhat startling conclusion, that the axioms of Euclid may be, perhaps, only approximately true'. His essay demonstrates the logical congruity of conceiving intelligent beings living on ellipsoids, on 'pseudospherical surfaces', in two dimensions or in four, while he concludes by pointing out that 'the axioms on which our geometrical system is based, are no necessary truths'; rather, they are 'the scientific expression of a most general fact of experience, the fact, namely, that in our space bodies can move freely without altering their form'.[9] Not what Alice experiences as she shrinks and swells, is crushed into the space of the Rabbit's house or finds her head swaying on an elongated neck in the canopy of a tree. In this alternative space and time her body's shape is not constant and its relation to its environment is merely approximate. Here the child's everyday and helpless experience of growing, and of being always the wrong size in a world designed by adults, is meshed with new mathematical speculations.

3. See David Landes, *Revolution in Time: Clocks and the Making of the Modern World*, Cambridge, MA, 1983.

4. See Wolfgang Schivelbusch, *The Railway Journey: The Industrialisation of Time and Space in the Nineteenth Century*, Berkeley, 1986.

5. Dan Falk, *In Search of Time: Journeys Along a Curious Dimension*, London, 2009, p. 72. 'Stevenson' refers to George Stephenson.

6. Philip Prodger, *Time Stands Still: Muybridge and the Instantaneous Photography Movement*, Stanford and New York, 2003.

7. Jimena Canales, *A Tenth of a Second: A History*, Chicago, 2009, pp. 25-29.

8. 'On the Methods of measuring very small portions of time, and their application to physiological purposes', *The London, Edinburgh and Dublin Philosophical Magazine and Journal of Science*, 4, 1853, p. 189.

9. *Academy*, vol. I, 1870, pp. 128–31.

Regularising time and defining ever smaller units were contemporary practices that chime with the age-old as well as up-to-date time-anxieties in *Alice*: 'Oh! The Duchess, the Duchess! Oh! *Wo'n't* she be savage if I've kept her waiting!' (p. 17). But industrial, scientific and technological changes are not the only markers of temporality in these books: sundials, solar time, dreams and tenses each add their diverse processes.

The wayward non-causal sequences experienced in dream nudge the episodes onward in both *Alice* books. Our daytime time-keeping is not the only possible way of experiencing the chronic – time in its extension. Dream shares with narrative the property of presenting experience as at once past and yet in process now. A book in Lewis Carroll's library, by the physician George Moore, dwells on just that quality of dream experience:

> During the interval between the evening and morning, what intricate visions of activity and interest, all according to some important law of our being, crowd upon the busy soul, not indeed in the distinctness of a measured and material succession, but as if at once past and yet present.[10]

10. George Moore, MD, *The Power of the Soul over the Body, Considered in Relation to Health and Morals*, New York, 1847, p. 74. He was a member of the Royal College of Physicians.

The temporal becomes spatial, with perspectives dissolved between past and present, all in the foreground and yet receding too. Moore goes on: 'There is no consciousness of time in our dreams; for a sense of time arises from a comparison of the relative duration of material changes, and therefore belongs only to the outward use of the mind.' Perhaps he means that it is impossible to recollect the length of time a dream takes to dream. It may seem endless and capable of unrolling aeons and yet flash past in a dreaming moment. It is certainly *not* the case in the *Alice* books that consciousness of time is obliterated: on the contrary, the anxiety of both books is propelled by a sense of haste and crowding.

But though dream is one kind of time-order in the Alice books, both books also explore the expansion and intricacy that games discover in time, whether the game be croquet or chess. Games complicate process and much of their enjoyment lies in that, but they also have a goal and therefore a control: in the Looking-Glass world Alice does eventually become a queen when as a pawn she reaches the end of the board. But that purposeful drive is subverted by the backwards order of things behind the looking-glass, where people are imprisoned before they commit a crime, the queen screams before she pricks herself, to approach things you must walk away and to stay in one place you must run fast:

> 'Well, in *our* country,' said Alice, still panting a little, 'You'd certainly get somewhere else – if you ran very fast for a long time as we've been doing.'
> 'A slow sort of country!' said the Queen. 'Now, *here*, you see, it takes all the running *you* can do, to keep in the same place. If you want to get somewhere else, you must run at least twice as fast as that.' (p. 143)

Carroll seems first to have conceived *Looking-Glass* on the plane of a chess-board and later added the optical reversing effects of the mirror: together they give rise to a conundrum that we recognise from his friend J.J. Sylvester's presidential address to the mathematical section of the 1866 British Association for the Advancement of Science:

> The laws of motion prove in a general way that the space we live in is a flat or level space (a 'homaloid'), our existence therein being assimilable to the life of a bookworm on a flat page: but what if the page were undergoing a process of gradual bending into a curved form? Mr. W.K. Clifford has indulged in some remarkable speculations as to the possibility of our being able to infer from certain unexplained phenomena of light and magnetism, the fact of our level space of three dimensions being in the act of undergoing in space of four dimensions (space as inconceivable to us as our space is to the book-worm) a distortion analogous to the rumpling of the page.[11]

11. J.J. Sylvester, 'Address to the Mathematical and Physical Section of the British Association', *Reports of the British Association for the Advancement of Science* (1869; published 1870), p. 4.

Placing the flat chess-board and the curved optics of the looking-glass together suggests a newly equivocal understanding of how time and space may be rumpled. In *Looking-Glass* particularly, Alice becomes aware that our mode of living in time is peculiar, and not necessarily the only pattern available: a thicker arrangement can be conceived. The White Queen recalls 'we had *such* a thunderstorm last Tuesday – I mean one of the last set of Tuesdays, you know'.

> Alice was puzzled. 'In *our* country,' she remarked, 'there's only one day at a time.'

> The Red Queen said, 'That's a poor thin way of doing things. Now *here*, we mostly have days and nights two or three at a time, and sometimes in winter we take as many as five nights together – for warmth, you know.' (p. 224)

This merging and crossing between different modalities of time helps to explain the attraction of *Alice* for the Surrealists: Dali's brilliant illustrations pithily express the dream-time of Alice. They show the child leaping and dancing, with her shifting shadow always at just the wrong angle to the sun. In *Wonderland* Alice unwarily shows off her knowledge of the earth's circling round the sun:

> 'If everybody minded their own business,' the Duchess said, in a hoarse growl, 'the world would go round a deal faster than it does.'
> 'Which would *not* be an advantage,' said Alice, who felt very glad to get an opportunity of showing off a little of her knowledge. 'Just think what work it would make with the day and night! You see the earth takes twenty-four hours to turn round on its axis – '
> 'Talking of axes,' said the duchess, 'chop off her head!' (p. 54)

The oral trumps the written. Indeed, throughout the two books tension is maintained between the oral, which is voiced *now* in the present, in a particular place, and the written, which always includes retrospect and may be carried anywhere. Dialogue is the primary medium of discourse in both books, dialogue which foregrounds the oral, springing back out of the written into the present of encounter.

Some of the more remarkable effects in *Alice* are quite customary in our experience now, one hundred and fifty-odd years later. The elision and flow from one scene into the next (queen into sheep, shop into river) correspond quite as much to the editing processes of cinema as to the motions of dream. Also, our familiarity with slow-motion photography may make Alice's leisurely fall into the underworld less astonishing, though the alternatives suggested by the narrator offer the deep absurdity of the choice that is no choice: 'Either the well was very deep or she fell very slowly, for she had plenty of time as she went down to look about her' (p. 10). A body falling down a well, however deep, is rarely leisurely.

The events of her fall mingle disappointment and good management:

> She took down a jar from one of the shelves as she passed: it was labelled 'ORANGE MARMALADE', but to her great disappointment it was empty: she did not like to drop the jar, for fear of killing someone underneath, so managed to put it in one of the cupboards as she fell past it. (p. 10)

Objects retain their lethal weight in motion even while Alice floats: gravity here is erratic in its action. Alice must be ten times as heavy as an empty marmalade jar, but in this instance she dawdles through the air while the jar threatens to plummet, reversing the usual error, mocked by John Stuart Mill, 'the belief that a body ten times as heavy as another falls ten times as fast'.[12]

12. John Stuart Mill, *A System Of Logic, Ratiocinative and Inductive: Being a Connected View of the Principles of Evidence, and the Methods of Scientific Investigation*, ed. J.M. Robson, 2 vols., in The Collected Works of John Stuart Mill, Toronto, 1973–74, vol. 8, p. 777.

13. James Joyce, *Finnegan's Wake* (1939), quoted in Roland McHugh, *Annotations to Finnegan's Wake*, Baltimore and London, 1991, p. 270.

Laws of motion had for the Victorians again become one of the most controversial aspects of time. The Hatter's tea-party, or capital-T party, combines the two. The argument there jumps up a notch from lower-case to upper-case 'T' as the Hatter claims Time as an ally. This move occurs when Alice is exasperated by the riddle without an answer: 'Why is a raven like a writing-desk?' The lack of an answer infringes all the rules of game time, so dear to Victorian middle-class culture: riddles rely on the pleasurable disappointment when the ingenious (but usually inadequate) answer is reached among the universe of possibilities. Here, nullity is all that occurs: no implosion or explosion of senses. Such a riddle also lacks closure, ebbing discomfitingly outward through time without stop. Time is stayed but trickles pointlessly. Samuel Beckett knows all about this peculiar time effect in his stage dialogue.

The puns in *Alice* lead also into *Finnegans Wake*: '*Though Wonderlawn's lost to us for ever. Alis, alas, she broke the glass! Liddell lokker through the leafery, ours is mistery of pain*'.[13] But the riddles without an answer lead into pure frustration for Alice.

> Alice sighed wearily. 'I think you might do something better with the time,' she said, 'than wasting it in asking riddles that have no answers.'
> 'If you knew Time as well as I do,' said the Hatter, 'you wouldn't talk about wasting *it*. It's *him*.'
> 'I don't know what you mean,' said Alice.
> 'Of course you don't!' the Hatter said, tossing his head contemptuously. 'I dare say you never even spoke to Time!'
> 'Perhaps not,' Alice cautiously replied, 'but I know I have to beat

, **I.** n. 1, *tempus*, *-ŏris*, n. *dies* (= the *patium* (= — as a period) † *aevum*, *in-m* (= interval), *aetas* (= age), *tempestas* on), *saeculum* (= a long —, a genera-*tium* (= leisure), *occasio*, *opportunitas* ortunity); the most **celebrated** general —, *clarissimus imperator suae aetatis* ; —, *nostrâ memoriâ* ; at the right —, (*tempori*, *temperi*) *ad tempus*, *tempestive*, ne, *in tempore*; in ancient —s, an-; from the — when, *ex quo* (*tempore*) ; at —, *omni tempore*; from — to —, *interdum* and then); for all —, *in omne tempus*; —, *mature* (e.g. to rise, *surgère*) ; against *sub* or *ad tempus* ; in the mean —, *interea*, ; according to — and circumstance, *pro et pro re*, *ex re et tempore*; to require — *pus postulare ad* ; it is — to go, *tempus ramus* or *ire* ; eight —s eight, *octo octies icata* ;

machination, n. = a secret, malicious de-sign, *machina*, *conatus*, *-ûs*, *dolus* ; to make —s, *consilia* (con)*coquère* ; to do a thing through anyone's —, *alqo auctore facère alqd.* **ma-chine**, n. *machina*, *machinatio*, *machinament-um* (= machinery) ; *compages*, *-is*, f. (= frame-work) ; the —, fabric of the human body, *com-pages corporis.* **machinery**, n. *machinatio*, *machinamenta, -orum*, n., *machinae*.

object, **I.** n. l, = something presented to the mind by the senses, *res*; the —s around us, *res externae*; to be the — of is variously rendered ; by *esse* and dat. (e.g. to be an — of care, hatred, contempt to anyone, *alci esse curae*, *odio*, *contemptui*), by *esse* and *in* (e.g. to be an — of hatred with anyone, *in odio esse apud alqm* ; to become an — of hatred, *in odium venire*, *per-venire*), by nouns already involving the idea (e.g. — of love, *amor*, *deliciae* ; — of desire, *desiderium*), by circumloc. with verbs (e.g. to be the of anyone's love, *ab alqo amari*, *diligi*) ;

top: Torsten Lauschmann
Digital Clock (Growing Zeros), 2010

bottom: Joseph Kosuth
Clock (One and Five), English/Latin version, 1965/1997

127

time when I learn music.'

'Ah! That accounts for it,' said the Hatter. 'He won't stand beating.' (pp. 61–2)

Personification scoops victory in the argument. Time, the Hatter claims, will work with you if you appreciate him: he will leap from nine in the morning to dinner time. But it turns out that the Hatter has quarrelled with Time and now they are stuck: 'It's always six o'clock now … it's always tea-time, and we've no time to wash the things between whiles.' 'Then you keep moving round, I suppose?' said Alice (p. 64). Instead of time moving, they must move round the table, as if on a clock face – and Alice very soon ends up with the March Hare's dirty tea-things in front of her (p. 66). The scene is tolerable because tea-time is not an instant but a period, so that the participants at the tea-party can continue their own lives and conversations within the arrested time. Six o'clock is understood here as tea-time, not as the moment of six pm. Indeed, the Hatter's watch 'tells the day of the month, and doesn't tell what o'clock it is'. The dream tea-time of the Hatter's tea-party is answered at the end of the book by Alice's older sister, who tells the newly woken Alice, 'It was a curious dream, dear, certainly; but now run in to your tea: it's getting late' (p. 109). The domestic round, time as diurnal family meal-times, prevails reassuringly at the close of *Wonderland*.

Only a very few years later than the *Alice* books, in 1874, Cantor argued in his theory of sets that there are degrees of infinity, even infinite infinities, and – for mathematicians – that eased the paradox of the continuity or discontinuity of motion. The teasing question of infinity or infinities is rapidly deflected by the March Hare:

'Then you keep moving round, I suppose?' said Alice.

'Exactly so,' said the Hatter: 'as the things get used up.'

'But what happens when you get to the beginning again?' Alice ventured to ask.

'Suppose we change the subject,' the March Hare interrupted, yawning. 'I'm getting tired of this.' (p. 64)

I am not a mathematician, so that for me, as for many readers, the key image of the Hatter's tea-party is of the endless tea-time and the dirty cups. But Alice can walk away; she is not imprisoned in their eternal loop (and, it turns out, neither are they, since the Hatter becomes a witness in the trial scene and in *Through the Looking-Glass* reappears as the Anglo-Saxon messenger Hatta).

This is not a systematic fiction. It is a field of play. Time here, as in a mathematical manifold, makes Euclidean sense only locally; the whole resists resolution. The various forms of time in the work will not lie still together; they are rumpled and energetic, endlessly alluring Alice.

– – –

A somewhat different and extended version of this essay has appeared in the *Modern Language Review* for October 2011 and I am grateful to the Modern Humanities Research Association for permission to publish here.

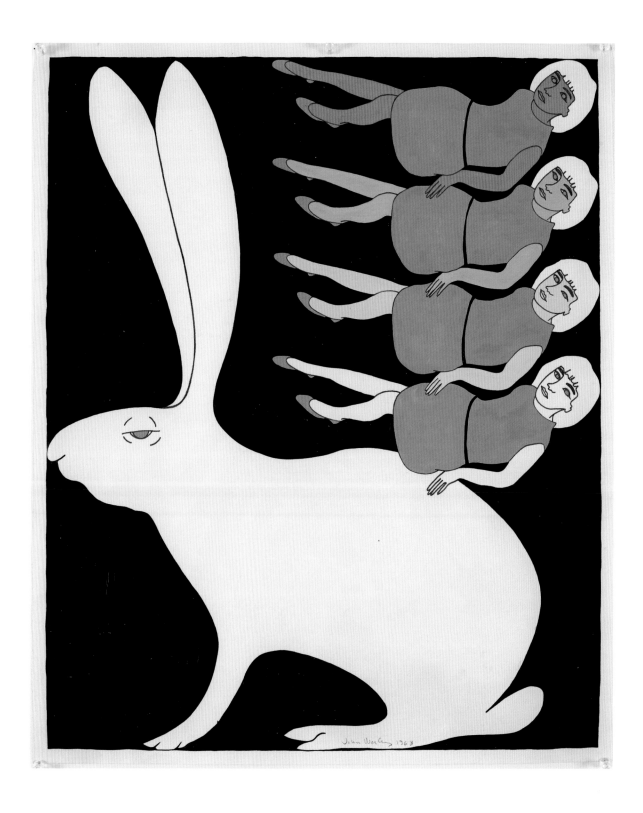

John Wesley
Untitled (Falling Alice), 1963

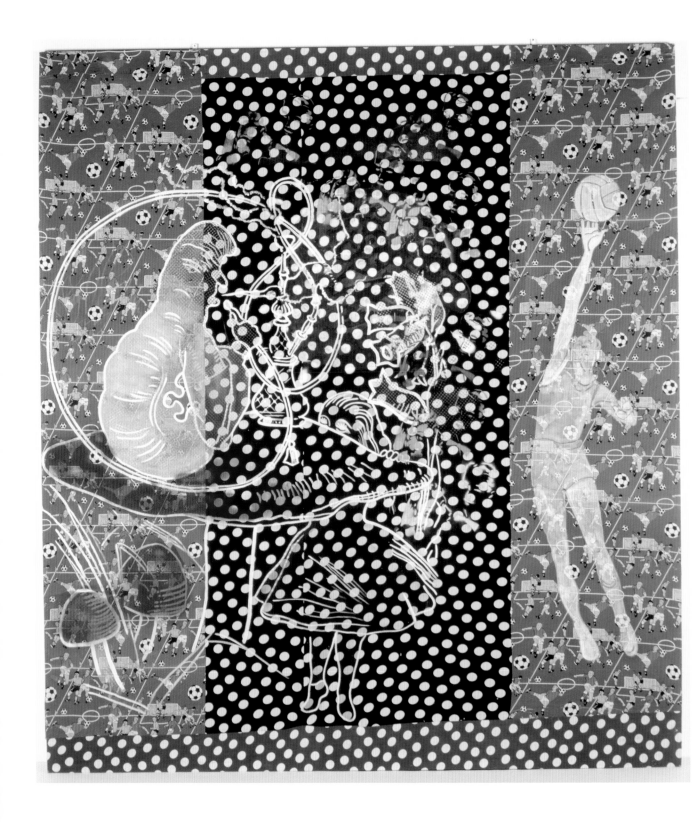

Sigmar Polke
Alice im Wunderland, 1971

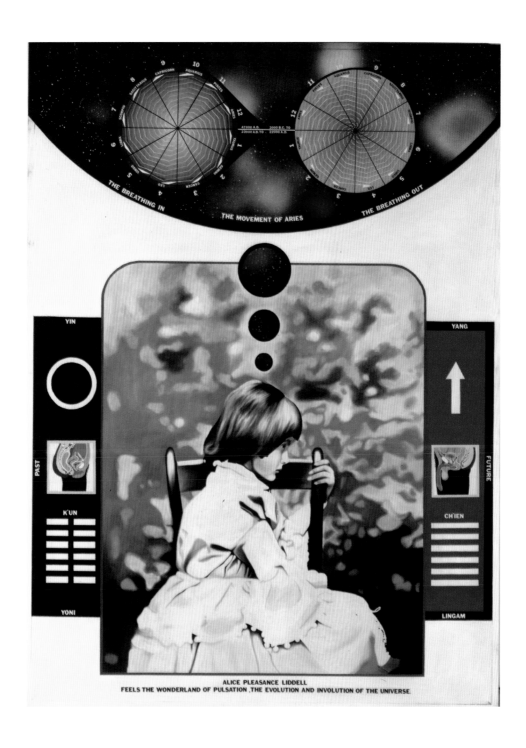

Paul Laffoley
Alice Pleasance Liddell, 1968

```
PRESS RELEASE FROM:
Yayoi Kusama
664 Avenue of the Americas
N.Y.,N.Y. 10010
242-5615
```

ALICE IN WONDERLAND

Featuring me,KUSAMA, mad as a hatter,and my troupe of nude dancers.

How about taking a trip with me out to Central Park where free tea will
be provided under the magic mushroom of the Alice in Wonderland Statue.
Alice was the grandmother of the Hippies.When she was low,Alice was the
first to take pills to make her high.
I,KUSAMA,AM THE MODERN ALICE IN WONDERLAND .

Like Alice,who went through the looking-glass,I,Kusama(who have lived
for years in my famous,specially-built room entirely covered by mirrors),
have opened up a world of fantasy and freedom.My world is peopled by a
group of real nude girl and boy dancers covered by genuine hand-painted
polka dots.You,too,can join my adventurous dance of life.

> Paint the beautiful blonde Lydia Lee.
> Paint your friends.
> Have your friends paint you.
> All together in the all-together.
> LOVE-LOVE-LOVE-LOVE-LOVE

Rendez-vous at the ALICE IN WONDERLAND Statue in Central Park,
Sunday,August 11,at 5:00 a.m.Because of the appropriate hour,
free tea will be provided.

My dancer's: Ernie Blake,Rick Erling,Lydia Lee,Ted Ryan,and Paul Sanford.

Yayoi Kusama
Alice in Wonderland Happening, 1968

This event took place at José de Creeft's sculpture of Alice in Wonderland
which was installed in Central Park in 1959.

left to right:
Adrian Piper
Alice Down the Rabbit Hole
The Mad Hatter's Tea Party
Alice and the Pack of Cards, 1966

134

Graham Ovenden
Alice, 1970

above:
'She kept on growing'

top right:
'But there isn't any wine'

bottom right:
'I don't think they play at all fairly'

Peter Blake
Illustrations to Through the Looking Glass, 1970

above left:
And to show I'm not proud you may shake hands with me!

above right:
So Alice picked him up very gently

right:
But isn't it old! Tweedledum cried

Duane Michals
Alice's Mirror, 1974

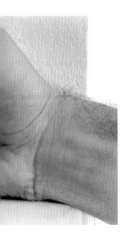

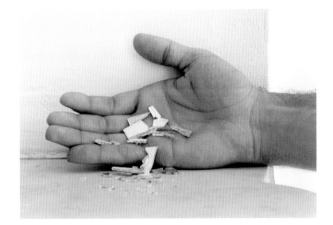

The Mind of James Joyce

1882-1941

The Turpitude of Lewis Carroll

1832-1898

The Turpitude of Oscar Wilde

1854-1900

The Mind of William Blake

1757-1827

The Turpitude of Charles Dodgson

1832-1898

The Dimension of Jonathan Swift

1667-1745

1809-1349	1832-1898	1667-1745
1757-1827	1882-1941	1854-1900
	1832-1898	

1973

The Dimension of Edgar Allan Poe

1809-1849

Marcel Broodthaers
Literary Paintings. English Series, 1972

VALIE EXPORT
Schriftzug Wien - Venedig, 1973

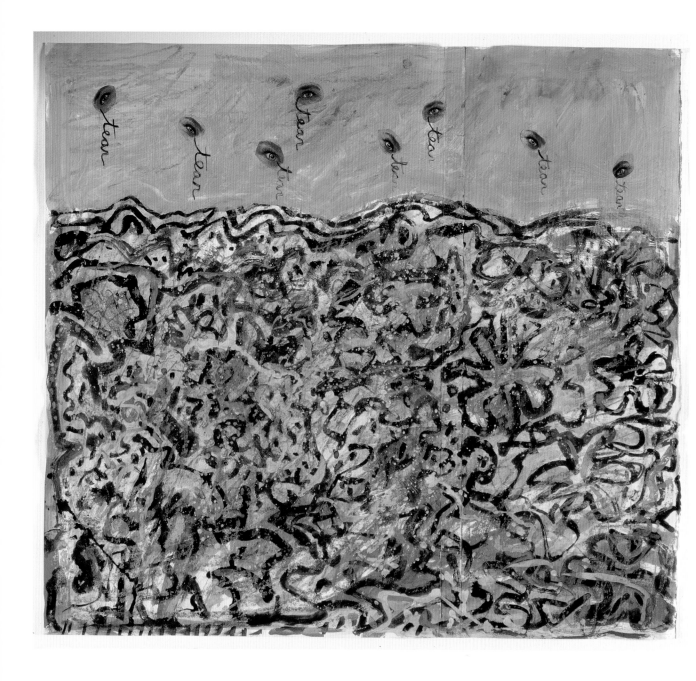

Robert Smithson
Untitled (Tear), 1961-63

Mel Bochner
Language is not transparent, 1969

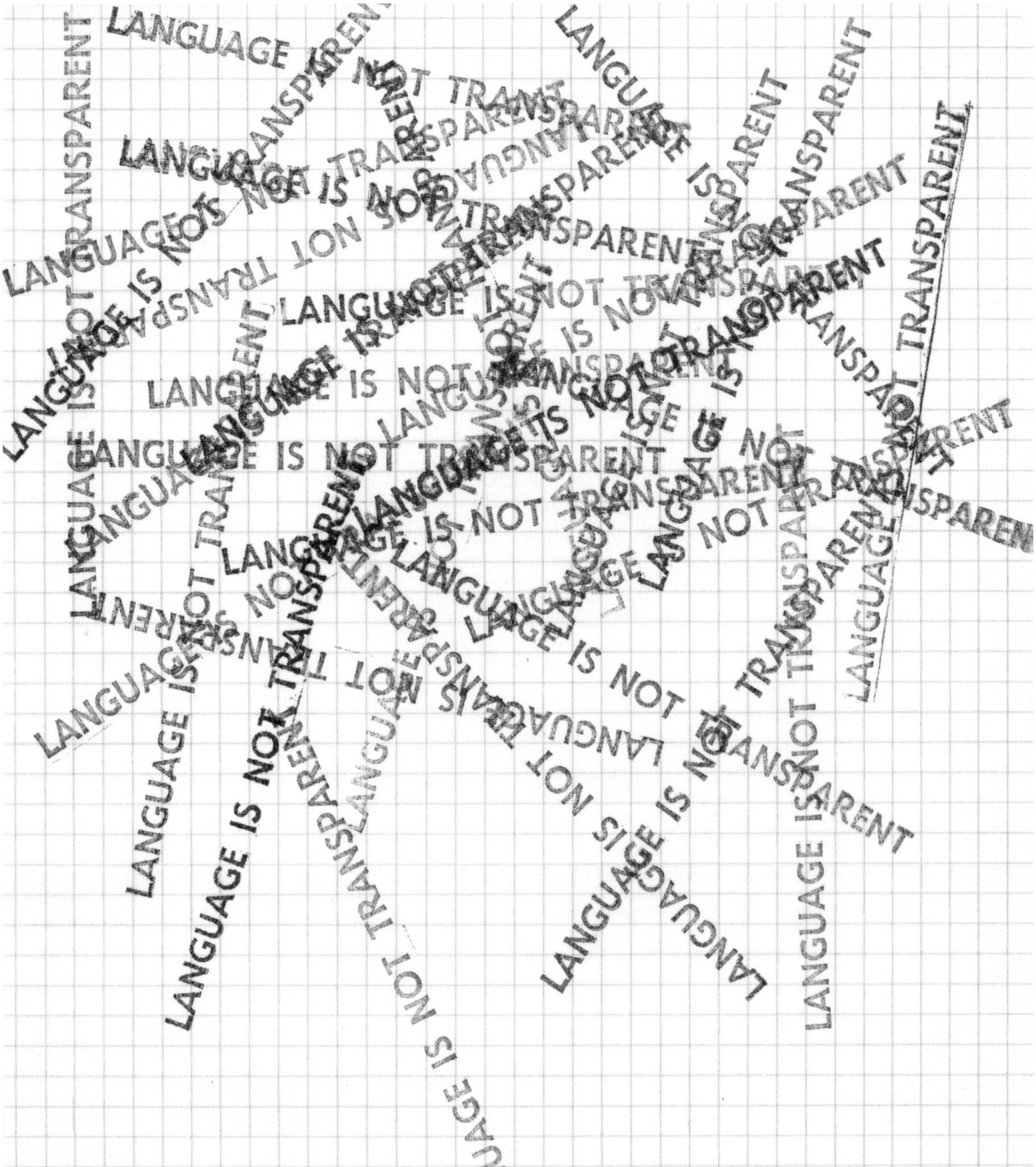
LANGUAGE IS NOT TRANSPARENT

AA Bronson
Through the Looking Glass, 2009

Francesca Woodman
Yet another leaden sky, Rome, 1977–78

Francesca Woodman
Untitled (Providence, Rhode Island) 1975–78

Allen Ruppersberg
The Never Ending Book, 2007

"CURIOUSER and curiouser!" cried
Alice (she was so much surprised,
that for the moment she quite for-
got how to speak good English);
I'm opening out like the largest telescope
that ever was! Good-bye, feet!" (for when
she looked down at her feet, they seemed
to be almost out of sight, they were getting so far off). "Oh, my poor little feet,
I wonder who will put on your shoes and
stockings for you now, dears? I'm sure
I sha'n't be able! I shall be a great deal
too far off to trouble myself about you:
you must manage the best way you can;
—but I must be kind to them," thought
Alice, " or perhaps they wo'n't walk the
way I want to go! Let me see: I'll give
them a new pair of boots every Christmas."
And she went on planning to herself
how she would

go by the carrier," she thought; " and how
funny it'll seem, sending presents to one's
own feet! And how
odd the directions will

lying down on one side, to look through
into the garden with one eye; but to get
through was more hopeless than ever: she
sat down and began to cry again.

Alice

Dinah. I th
if you could
dear quiet th
herself, as s

pool, "and
the fire, lick
face — and s
to nurse — a
catching mice — oh, I beg your pardon!"
cried Alice again, for this time the Mouse
was bristling all over, and she felt certain
it must be really offended. " We wo'n't
talk about her any more, if you'd rather not."
[32]

I ca'n't remember half of them — and it
belongs to a farmer, you know, and he
says it's so useful, it's worth a hundred
pounds! He says it kills all the rats and
— oh dear!" cried Alice in a sorrowful
[33]

Eaglet, and several other curious creatures.
Alice led the way, and the whole party
swam to the shore.

[34]

150   Tim Rollins
       White Alice III, 1992

waiting!"—Alice felt so desperate that she
was ready to ask help of any one; so,
when the Rabbit came near her, she began, in a low, timid voice, "If you please,
Sir——" The Rabbit started violently,

as herself, to see if she could have been
changed for any of them.
"I'm sure I'm not Ada," she said, "for
her hair goes in such long ringlets, and

began to repeat it, but her voice sounded
hoarse and strange, and the words did not
come the same as they used to do:—

    "*How doth the little crocodile*

. . . . *the Nile*

. . . . *to grin,*
. . . . *claws,*
. . . . *in,*
. . . . *!*"

. . . . . . at the right
. . . . . . her eyes filled
. . . . . on, "I must
. . . . . all have to go
. . . . . e house, and
. . . . . lay with, and
. . . . . learn! No,
. . . . . it: if I'm
. . . . . It'll be no
. . . . . ds down and
. . . . . ar!' I shall
. . . . . am I, then?

. . . . *ears*

. . . . . spades, then
. . . . . behind them
. . . . . e soon made

. . . . . pool of tears
. . . . . she was nine

. . . . . much!" said
. . . . . rying to find
. . . . . nished for it
. . . . . owned in my
. . . . . er thing, to be
. . . . . queer to-day."
. . . . . ing splashing

. . . . . *ng Tale*

. . . . . Silence all
. . . . am the Con-
. . . . oured by the
. . . . . to by the
. . . . nd had been
. . . . o usurpation
. . . . Morcar, the
. . . . bria——'"
. . . . th a shiver.
. . . . d the Mouse,
. . . . "Did you

. . . . astily.
. . . . the Mouse,
. . . . r, the earls of
. . . . ared for him:
. . . . e archbishop

. . . . better. And this Alice would not allow,
without knowing how old it was, and, as
the Lory positively refused to tell its age,
there was no more to be said.
At last the Mouse, who seemed to be a

Alice kept her eyes anxiously fixed on it,
for she felt sure she would catch a bad
cold if she did not get dry very soon.
"Ahem!" said the Mouse with an
important air. "Are you all ready? This

of Canterbury, found it advisable——'"
"Found *what?*" said the Duck.
"Found *it*," the Mouse replied rather
crossly: "of course you know what 'it'
means."

[37]   [38]   [39]

Anna Gaskell
Untitled #5 (Wonder), 1996

top right: Anna Gaskell
Untitled #6 (Wonder), 1996

bottom right: Anna Gaskell
Untitled #8 (Wonder), 1996

Luc Tuymans
Wonderland, 2007

Fiona Banner
Arsewoman in Wonderland Act I, 2001

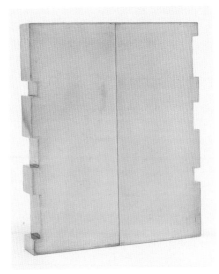

Rodney Graham
Alice's Adventures in Wonderland, 1989

Bill Woodrow
English Heritage – Humpty Fucking Dumpty, 1987

Kiki Smith
Pool of Tears 2 (after Lewis Carroll), 2000

Kiki Smith
Come Away From Her (after Lewis Carroll), 2003

Nalini Malani
Alice, 2006

right: Yifat Bezalel
A Broken Hill, 2010

162

Gary Hill
Why do things get in a muddle? (Come on Petunia), 1984

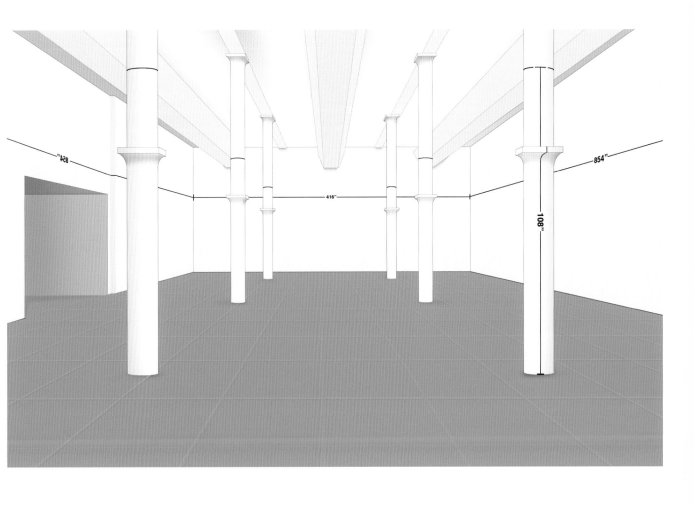

Mel Bochner
Installation design for *Measurement: Eye-Level Perimeter
(Ask Alice)*, 1969/2011

Diana Thater
The Caucus Race, 1998

right: Liliana Porter
Sea Side (detail), 1989

Jason Rhoades
Tate Touche from My Madinah: in pursuit of my ermitage, 2004

right: Pierre Huyghe
A Smile Without a Cat, 2002

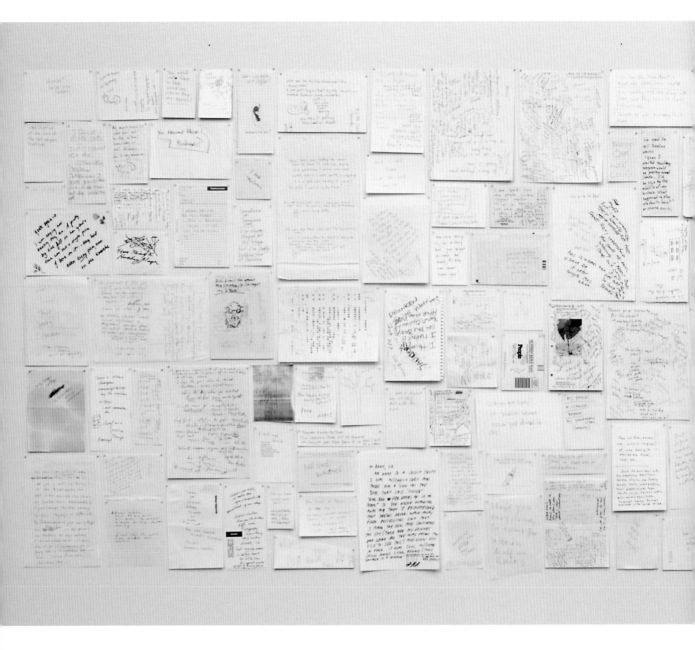

Joseph Grigely
167 White Conversations, 2004

170

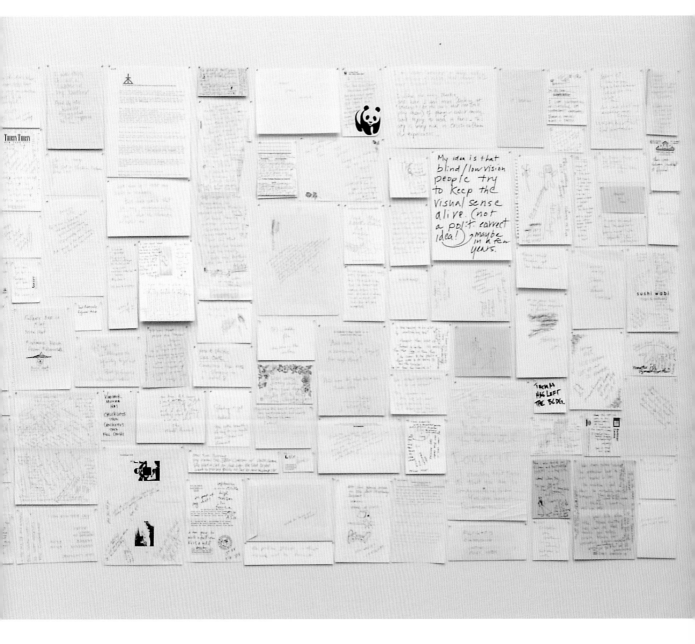

left: Douglas Gordon
Through a Looking Glass, 1999

Dan Graham
Girl's Make-up Room, 1998-2000

Michelle Stuart
The other side of the glass, 2010

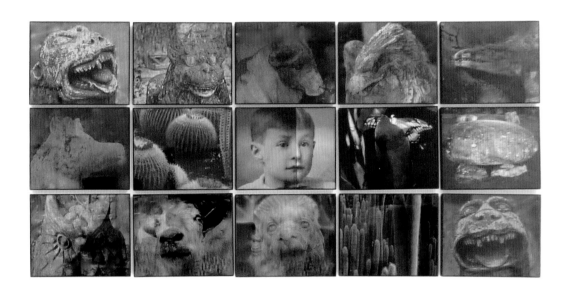

176   Annalies Štrba
Nyima 438, 2009

List of works

List of exhibited works in chronological order
Measurements of artworks are given in millimetres, height
before width.

Ottewill Folding Box Camera 1853
Whole-plate collapsible field camera, made entirely of wood
National Media Museum, Bradford

Unknown photographer
Charles L. Dodgson 1852-1860
Albumen print
Image: 197 x 146 mm
Lent by the National Portrait Gallery, London

Christ Church photograph album
The Governing Body of Christ Church, Oxford

Charles L. Dodgson 1832-1898
Scrapbook with newspaper cuttings ('Lewis Carroll Scrapbook') 1855-72
Print on paper
Rare Books and Special Collections Division, Library of Congress,
Washington, D. C.

William Holman Hunt 1827-1910
Study for 'The Finding of the Saviour in the Temple' 1856
Pencil and chalk on paper
Support: 711 x 508 mm
Tate Collection, presented by A.W.F. Fuller 1941

Charles L. Dodgson 1832-1898
Charles L. Dodgson July/August 1857
First generation reproduction of original print
Edward Wakeling and the Lewis Carroll Society

Charles L. Dodgson 1832-1898
Hallam Tennyson 28 September 1857
First generation reproduction of original print
Edward Wakeling and the Lewis Carroll Society

Charles L. Dodgson 1832-1898
'Little Red Riding-Hood' 18 August 1857
First generation reproduction of original print
Edward Wakeling and the Lewis Carroll Society

Charles L. Dodgson 1832-1898
The New Book July/August 1857
First generation reproduction of original print
Edward Wakeling and the Lewis Carroll Society

Charles L. Dodgson 1832-1898
The Broad Walk, Oxford Spring 1857
First generation reproduction of original print
Edward Wakeling and the Lewis Carroll Society

Charles L. Dodgson 1832-1898
Reginald Southey and Skeletons June 1857
First generation reproduction of original print
Edward Wakeling and the Lewis Carroll Society

Charles L. Dodgson 1832-1898
Lorina Charlotte Liddell; Alice Pleasance Liddell; Edith Mary Liddell
1858-1860
Albumen prints, triptych
100 x 76 mm
National Portrait Gallery, London, purchased jointly with the National
Museum of Photography, Film and Television, Bradford, through The
Art Fund and the National Heritage Memorial Fund, 2002

Charles L. Dodgson 1832-1898
Alice Pleasance Liddell Summer 1858
Modern print from whole-plate glass negative
152 x 127 mm
National Portrait Gallery, London, purchased jointly with the National
Museum of Photography, Film and Television, Bradford, with help from
the National Heritage Memorial Fund, 2002

Charles L. Dodgson 1832-1898
*Edith Mary Liddell; Lorina Charlotte ('Ina') Liddell; Alice Pleasance
Liddell* Summer 1858
Modern print from whole-plate glass negative
156 x 176 mm
National Portrait Gallery, London, purchased jointly with the National
Museum of Photography, Film and Television, Bradford, through The
Art Fund and the National Heritage Memorial Fund, 2002

Charles L. Dodgson 1832-1898
Alice Liddell as the 'Beggar-Maid' Summer 1858
First generation reproduction of original print
Edward Wakeling and the Lewis Carroll Society

Charles L. Dodgson 1832-1898
*Edith Mary Liddell; Lorina Charlotte ('Ina') Liddell; Alice Pleasance
Liddell* July 1860
Modern print from whole-plate glass negative
254 x 203 mm
National Portrait Gallery, London, purchased jointly with the National
Museum of Photography, Film and Television, Bradford, through The
Art Fund and the National Heritage Memorial Fund, 2002

Charles L. Dodgson's Wet-Collodion Photographic Outfit c. 1860
340 x 320 x 250 mm
Mixed media
Museum of the History of Science, University of Oxford

Hills and Saunders active 1850-1900
Lewis Carroll (Charles L. Dodgson) 1860s
Albumen print
85 x 57 mm
Lent by the National Portrait Gallery, London

Unknown Artist, British School
Alexander Macmillan 1860s
Lithograph
450 x 342 mm
Lent by the National Portrait Gallery, London

Charles L. Dodgson 1832-1898
Alice Pleasance Liddell Spring 1860
Modern print from whole-plate glass negative
126 x 152 mm
National Portrait Gallery, London, purchased jointly with the National
Museum of Photography, Film and Television, Bradford, with help from
the National Heritage Memorial Fund, 2002

Charles L. Dodgson 1832-1898
Alice and Lorina Liddell May or June 1860
First generation reproduction of original print
Edward Wakeling and the Lewis Carroll Society

Charles L. Dodgson 1832-1898
Glass Negative of Alice Liddell Wearing a Garland May or June 1860
Wet Collodian on glass negative, number 561 by photographer in the
emulsion
153 x 128 mm
Private Collection, New York

Charles L. Dodgson 1832-1898
William Holman Hunt 30 June 1860
First generation reproduction of original print
Edward Wakeling Collection

Charles L. Dodgson 1832-1898
William Holman Hunt 30 June 1860
First generation reproduction of original print
Edward Wakeling and the Lewis Carroll Society

Charles L. Dodgson 1832-1898
Alice Pleasance Liddell July 1860
Albumen print
95 x 54 mm
National Portrait Gallery, London, purchased jointly with the National
Museum of Photography, Film, and Television, Bradford, through The
Art Fund and the National Heritage Memorial Fund, 2002

Charles L. Dodgson 1832-1898
Alice Liddell July 1860
First generation reproduction of original print
Edward Wakeling and the Lewis Carroll Society

Happy Families, The New and Diverting Game for Juveniles 1860
Print on card
99 x 76 x 24 mm
V&A Museum of Childhood, Victoria and Albert Museum, London

Charles L. Dodgson 1832-1898
Magdalen Tower, Oxford June 1861
First generation reproduction of original print
Edward Wakeling and the Lewis Carroll Society

Charles L. Dodgson 1832-1898
The Liddell children 1862
Watercolour on paper
Framed: 67 x 99 mm
Collection of Charlie Lovett, Winston-Salem, N. C., USA

Charles L. Dodgson 1832-1898
Margaret Dodgson in 'The Reflection' September 1862
First generation reproduction of original print
Edward Wakeling and the Lewis Carroll Society

Charles L. Dodgson 1832-1898
Lewis Carroll's Diaries, Vol IV (no. 8) 9 May 1862-6 September 1864
Paper. Contemporary foliation by the author. Brown or green board
bindings with cloth spines.
183 x 115 mm
British Library, by kind permission of the C. L. Dodgson Estate

Arthur Hughes 1832-1915
The Lady with the Lilacs 1863
Oil on canvas
445 x 225 mm
Collection Art Gallery of Ontario, Toronto. Presented in memory of
Frances Baines, Membership Secretary (1951-1964), by members of
the Council, the Women's Committee and staff of the Art Gallery of
Toronto, 1966

Charles L. Dodgson 1832-1898
Agnes Hughes asleep on a couch 1863
Mounted Albumen photographic print
Tate Library and Archive

Charles L. Dodgson 1832-1898
Agnes Hughes standing in front of a wall 1863
Mounted Albumen photographic print
Tate Library and Archive

Charles L. Dodgson 1832-1898
Amy and Agnes Hughes asleep on a couch 1863
Mounted Albumen photographic print
Tate Library and Archive

Charles L. Dodgson 1832-1898
Arthur Hughes and his Daughter Agnes 12 October 1863
Mounted Albumen photographic print
Tate Library and Archive

Charles L. Dodgson 1832-1898
The Four Rossettis 7 October 1863
First generation reproduction of original print
Edward Wakeling and the Lewis Carroll Society

Charles L. Dodgson 1832-1898
Dante Gabriel Rossetti 6 October 1863
First generation reproduction of original print
Edward Wakeling and the Lewis Carroll Society

Charles L. Dodgson 1832-1898
Alexander Munro and Wife 7 October 1863
First generation reproduction of original print
Edward Wakeling and the Lewis Carroll Society

Charles L. Dodgson 1832-1898
Dante Gabriel Rossetti 6 October 1863
First generation reproduction of original print
Edward Wakeling and the Lewis Carroll Society

Charles L. Dodgson 1832-1898
The Dream 1863
Albumen print
250 x 190 mm
The Royal Photographic Society Collection at the National Media
Museum, Bradford

Charles L. Dodgson 1832-1898
George MacDonald and Lily 14 October 1863
First generation reproduction of original print
Edward Wakeling and the Lewis Carroll Society

Charles L. Dodgson 1832-1898
Amy Hughes 12 October 1863
First generation reproduction of original print
Edward Wakeling and the Lewis Carroll Society

Charles L. Dodgson 1832-1898
Arthur Hughes 12 October 1863
First generation reproduction of original print
Edward Wakeling and the Lewis Carroll Society

Charles L. Dodgson 1832-1898
Lewis Carroll diaries Vol. V (number 9) 13 September 1864-24
January 1868
Paper. Contemporary foliation by the author. Brown or green board
bindings with cloth spines
183 x 115 mm
British Library, by kind permission of the C. L. Dodgson Estate

Charles L. Dodgson 1832-1898
Original Drawing for 'Alice in Wonderland'
Ink on paper
The Governing Body of Christ Church, Oxford

Charles L. Dodgson 1832-1898
Original Drawing of Rabbits
Ink on paper
The Governing Body of Christ Church, Oxford

Charles L. Dodgson 1832-1898
Original Drawing of the Pool of Tears
Ink on paper
The Governing Body of Christ Church, Oxford

Charles L. Dodgson 1832-1898
Original Drawing of Giant Puppy
Ink on paper
The Governing Body of Christ Church, Oxford

Charles L. Dodgson 1832-1898
Original Drawing - sketch of Alice with Ostrich
Ink on paper
The Governing Body of Christ Church, Oxford

Charles L. Dodgson 1832-1898
Original Drawing - sketch of the Caterpillar
Ink on paper
The Governing Body of Christ Church, Oxford

Charles L. Dodgson 1832-1898
Original Drawing of Heads
Ink on paper
The Governing Body of Christ Church, Oxford

Charles L. Dodgson 1832-1898
Original Drawing - sketch of the Mock Turtle and Griffin
Ink on paper
The Governing Body of Christ Church, Oxford

Wilfred Dodgson 1834-1914
Original Drawing - sketch of Mock Turtle
Ink on paper
The Governing Body of Christ Church, Oxford

Wilfred Dodgson 1834-1914
Original Drawing - sketch of the Griffin
Ink on paper
The Governing Body of Christ Church, Oxford

Charles L. Dodgson 1832-1898
Alice's Adventures Underground 1864
Original manuscript
British Library, by kind permission of the C. L. Dodgson Estate

Sir John Tenniel 1820-1914
Punch cover, Vol 46 1864
Print on paper
Edward Wakeling Collection

Dante Gabriel Rossetti 1828-1882
The Beloved ('The Bride') 1865-6
Oil on canvas
825 x 762 mm (frame: 1220 x 110 x 83 mm)
Tate Collection, purchased with assistance from Sir Arthur Du Cros Bt
and Sir Otto Beit KCMG through the Art Fund 1916

Sir John Everett Millais 1829-1896
Waking 1865
Oil on canvas
870 x 670 mm (frame: 1206 x 1002 mm)
Perth Museum & Art Gallery, Perth & Kinross Council, Scotland

Charles L. Dodgson 1832-1898
John Everett Millais 21 July 1865
First generation reproduction of original print
Edward Wakeling and the Lewis Carroll Society

Charles L. Dodgson 1832-1898
Mary Millais in 'Waking' 21 July 1865
First generation reproduction of original print
Edward Wakeling and the Lewis Carroll Society

Charles L. Dodgson 1832-1898
Plan of the illustrations for "Alice's Adventures in Wonderland"
Indigo ink on paper
The Governing Body of Christ Church, Oxford

Sir John Tenniel 1820-1914
A little door about fifteen inches high 1865
Pencil on paper
70 x 80 mm
Rosenbach Museum & Library, Philadelphia

Sir John Tenniel 1820-1914
The Pool of Tears 1865
Pencil on paper
70 x 100 mm
Rosenbach Museum & Library, Philadelphia

Arthur Hughes 1832-1915
Portrait of Mrs Leathart and Her Three Children 1863-1866
Oil on canvas
547 x 927 mm
Tyne & Wear Archives & Museums

Charles L. Dodgson 1832-1898
Plan of the illustrations for "Through the Looking Glass"
Indigo ink on paper
The Governing Body of Christ Church, Oxford

Sir John Tenniel 1820-1914
The Jabberwocky with eyes of flame 1870-71
Pencil on paper
170 x 100 mm
Rosenbach Museum & Library, Philadelphia

Sir John Tenniel 1820-1914
A dissolving view 1870-71
Pencil on paper
120 x 100 mm
Rosenbach Museum & Library, Philadelphia

The Dalziel Brothers
Printing woodblocks from first edition of "Alice in Wonderland"
Selection of ten
Various sizes
British Library, by kind permission of the C. L. Dodgson Estate

Original metal printing blocks of Tenniel's illustrations of Alice in
Wonderland 1865
Selection of five
Metal (Electrotype)
Thomas and Greta Schuster

Frontispiece for the compositions for Alice in Wonderland,
by William Boyd
1870
200 x 300 mm
Edward Wakeling Collection

Charles L. Dodgson 1832-1898
Alice Pleasance Liddell 25 June 1870
Albumen carte-de-visite
91 x 58 mm
National Portrait Gallery, London, purchased jointly with the National
Museum of Photography, Film and Television, Bradford, through The
Art Fund and the National Heritage Memorial Fund, 2002

Julia Margaret Cameron 1815-1879
The Sisters – Edith and Alice Liddell 1870
Print on paper
200 x 335 mm
The Royal Photographic Society Collection at the National Media
Museum, Bradford

Julia Margaret Cameron 1815-1879
Claud and Lady Florence Anson 1870-78
Print on paper
280 x 342 mm
The Royal Photographic Society Collection at the National Media
Museum, Bradford

Julia Margaret Cameron 1815-1879
St Agnes (Alice Liddell) 1872
Print on paper
227 x 340 mm
The Royal Photographic Society Collection at the National Media
Museum, Bradford

Julia Margaret Cameron 1815-1879
Lorina, Edith and Alice Liddell 1872
Print on paper
380 x 486 mm
The Royal Photographic Society Collection at the National Media
Museum, Bradford

Julia Margaret Cameron 1815-1879
Lorina, Edith and Alice Liddell 1872
Print on paper
275 x 330 mm
The Royal Photographic Society Collection at the National Media
Museum, Bradford

Julia Margaret Cameron 1815-1879
Venus Chiding Cupid and Removing His Wings 1872
Albumen print
260 x 300 mm (mounted: 500 x 650 mm)
The Royal Photographic Society Collection at the National Media
Museum, Bradford

Julia Margaret Cameron 1815-1879
Pomona 1872-79
Albumen print
260 x 300 mm (mounted 508 x 609 mm)
The Royal Photographic Society Collection at the National Media
Museum, Bradford

Sir John Tenniel 1820-1914
'The Monster Slain' caricature in Punch 16 March 1872
Print on paper
Edward Wakeling Collection

Charles Handel Rand Marriott 1839-1889
Wonderland Quadrilles 1872
Print on paper
337 x 255 mm
Collection of Charlie Lovett, Winston-Salem, N.C., USA

Charles Handel Rand Marriott 1831-1889
The Looking Glass Quadrille
Print on paper
347 x 250 mm
Collection of Charlie Lovett, Winston-Salem, N.C., USA

Charles L. Dodgson 1832-1898
'A Tea Merchant' 14 July 1873
First generation reproduction of original print
Edward Wakeling and the Lewis Carroll Society

Charles L. Dodgson 1832-1898
John Ruskin 3 June 1875
First generation reproduction of original print
Edward Wakeling and the Lewis Carroll Society

Charles L. Dodgson 1832-1898
St. George and the Dragon 26 June 1875
First generation reproduction of original print
Edward Wakeling and the Lewis Carroll Society

Alexander Bassano 1809-1913
Alice, Edith and Ina Liddell c. 1876
Albumen print, mounted as a cabinet card
Image: 148 x 100 mm
Support: 167 x 107 mm
Private Collection, courtesy of Hans P. Kraus, Jr., New York

George Dunlop Leslie 1835-1921
Alice in Wonderland 1879
Oil on canvas
814 x 1118 mm
The Royal Pavilion & Museums, Brighton & Hove

Sir John Tenniel 1820-1914
'Alice in Blunderland' caricature in Punch 30 October 1880
Print on paper
Edward Wakeling Collection

William Holman Hunt 1827-1910
The Triumph of the Innocents 1883-4
Oil on canvas
1562 x 2540 mm (framed: 2208 x 3175 x 125 mm)
Tate Collection, presented by Sir John Middlemore Bt 1918

*Theatre Poster of "Alice in Wonderland" in the Prince of Wales Theatre
1886* 1886
575 x 423 x 23 mm
V&A Theatre and Performance

*Theatre Programme of "Alice in Wonderland" in the Prince of Wales
Theatre 1886* 1886
175 x 122 mm
V&A Theatre and Performance

*Photograph of the 1886 Henry Saville Clark Production of Alice in
Wonderland*
1886
Framed: 200 x 350 mm
Edward Wakeling Collection

*Proof Sheets from 1886 facsimile edition of the manuscript of "Alice's
Adventures Underground": Dedication page, p.13, p. 23, p.33, p.37,
p.46, p.49, p.76, p.86, The Mouse's Tale*
Print on paper
The Governing Body of Christ Church, Oxford

*Proof Sheet for "Alice in Wonderland" Macmillan printed edition with
additional drawing*
Ink and print on paper
The Governing Body of Christ Church, Oxford

Charles L. Dodgson 1832-1898
*Proof sheet of the Mouse's Tale, cut up and re-pasted by Dodgson
in a curve*
Print on paper, glue
The Governing Body of Christ Church, Oxford

Charles L. Dodgson 1832-1898
*Straight proof sheet for the Mouse's Tale from the Macmillan
printed edition*
Print on paper
The Governing Body of Christ Church, Oxford

Charles L. Dodgson 1832-1898
Alice's Adventures Underground 1886
Facsimile of the original manuscript
Published by MacMillan
Edward Wakeling Collection

Sir John Tenniel 1820-1914
Caricature based on illustrations of 'Alice's Adventures in Wonderland'
in Punch 26 February 1887
Print on paper
Edward Wakeling Collection

Globe Theatre programme of "Alice in Wonderland" 1888 1888
210 x 95 mm (closed)
V&A Theatre and Performance

Globe Theatre programme of "Alice in Wonderland" 1888 December
1888
210 x 280 mm (open)
V&A Theatre and Performance

Alice in Wonderland stamp cases 1890 (1911 version)
Print on paper
Thomas and Greta Schuster

Alice in Wonderland stamp case 1890 (1911 version)
Print on paper
Thomas and Greta Schuster

Royal Doulton Cheshire Cat c. 1890
Salt-glazed stoneware
400 x 800 x 400 mm
Thomas and Greta Schuster

Theatre programme of "Alice in Wonderland", Opera Comique,
December 1898 December 1898
253 x 157 mm
V&A Theatre and Performance

Cutting of "Alice in Wonderland" at Opera Comique in The Daily
Graphic, December 1898 December 1898
575 x 423 x 23 mm
V&A Theatre and Performance

Souvenir programme of "Alice in Wonderland" at Opera Comique,
100th Performance, 1898 1898
246 x 184 mm
V&A Theatre and Performance

Hubert von Herkomer 1849-1914
Posthumous portrait of Lewis Carroll 1898
Oil on canvas
750 x 625 mm (framed: 1045 x 920 mm)
By permission of the Governing Body of Christ Church, Oxford

Two joined pages of the Sketch, "Alice in Wonderland" at Opera
Comique, January 1899 January 1899
577 x 787 x 23 mm
V&A Theatre and Performance

Images from "Alice in Wonderland" at Vaudeville, in the Illustrated
Sporting and Dramatic News, December 29 1900 29 December 1900
575 x 423 x 23 mm
V&A Theatre and Performance

Photographs from "Alice in Wonderland" at Vaudeville, in The Sketch,
December 1900 December 1900
575 x 423 x 23 mm
V&A Theatre and Performance

Ellaline Terris as Alice
From the Vaudeville Theatre production of Alice in Wonderland, 1900
325 x 188 mm
Collection of Charlie Lovett, Winston-Salem, N.C., USA

Programme from Alice in Wonderland at The Vaudeville Theatre,
London 1900
256 x 115 mm
Collection of Charlie Lovett, Winston-Salem, N.C., USA

Alice in Wonderland magic lantern slide – set of 24 1900-1925
Magic lantern slide
Each: 80 x 80 x 4 mm
Courtesy of The Bill Douglas Centre for The History of Cinema and
Popular Culture, University of Exeter

Magic lantern 1900-1925
Metal
Courtesy of The Bill Douglas Centre for The History of Cinema and
Popular Culture, University of Exeter

Mazzawattee Tea Tins c. 1895
3 sizes (1 lbs, 3lbs, 10lbs)
Thomas and Greta Schuster

Articulated 'Alice' related painted wooden figures c. 1900
Painted plywood
Height: 50-160 mm
Thomas and Greta Schuster

Harry Furniss 1854-1925
Lewis Carroll (Charles L. Dodgson) before 1902
Pen and ink on paper
273 x 191 mm
Lent by the National Portrait Gallery, London

Harry Furniss 1854-1925
Lewis Carroll (Charles L. Dodgson)
Pen and ink on paper
210 x 133 mm
Lent by the National Portrait Gallery, London

Harry Furniss 1854-1925
Lewis Carroll (Charles L. Dodgson)
Pen and ink on paper
184 x 102 mm
Lent by the National Portrait Gallery, London

Cecil Hepworth and Percy Stow
Alice in Wonderland 1903
Black and white film, silent
9.35 min
Courtesy of British Film Institute

First Alice in Wonderland crockery set Sold in Harrod's 1906
Martien Levien Porcelain, printed by lithographic transfer and finished
by hand
Various sizes
Thomas and Greta Schuster

Programme of "Alice in Wonderland", Empire Liverpool, 1911 1911
249 x 126 mm
V&A Theatre and Performance

Alexander Bassano 1809-1913
Estelle Dudley as Alice in 'Alice in Wonderland' 14 December 1917
Print from whole-plate glass negative
Lent by the National Portrait Gallery, London

Alexander Bassano 1809-1913
Estelle Dudley as Alice in 'Alice in Wonderland' 14 December 1917
Print from whole-plate glass negative
Lent by the National Portrait Gallery, London

Alexander Bassano 1809-1913
Charles Hayden Coffin as the Mad Hatter in 'Alice in Wonderland';
Estelle Dudley as Alice in 'Alice in Wonderland' 14 December 1917
Print from whole-plate glass negative
Lent by the National Portrait Gallery, London

Alexander Bassano 1809-1913
Estelle Dudley as Alice in 'Alice in Wonderland' 14 December 1917
Print from whole-plate glass negative
Lent by the National Portrait Gallery, London

Alexander Bassano 1809-1913
Estelle Dudley as Alice in 'Alice in Wonderland', with boy actor as the
White Rabbit 1917
Print from whole-plate glass negative
Lent by the National Portrait Gallery, London

Alexander Bassano 1809-1913
Estelle Dudley as Alice in 'Alice in Wonderland' with boy actor as the
Cat 14 December 1917
Print from whole-plate glass negative
Lent by the National Portrait Gallery, London

The New and Diverting Game of Alice in Wonderland 1918
98 x 67 x 25 mm
Printed card
V&A Museum of Childhood

Charles Francis Annesley Voysey 1857-1941
Alice in Wonderland c. 1920
Furnishing fabric
1470 x 1050 x 50 mm
Victoria and Albert Museum, London. Given by J.W.F. Morton

Walt Disney 1901-1966
Alice's Wonderland 1923
Black and white film, silent
8.05 minutes
Artwork provided courtesy of Animation Research Library, Walt Disney
Animation Studios, Burbank, California

Tony Sarg 1880-1942
'Alice and Wonderland" Wallpaper 1930s
Colour printed wallpaper
800 x 550 mm section
Thomas and Greta Schuster

Eileen Agar 1899-1991
Three Symbols 1930
Oil on canvas
1003 x 559 mm (framed: 1100 x 650 x 60 mm)
Tate Collection. Purchased 1964

Paul Nash 1889-1946
Harbour and Room 1932-36
Oil on canvas
914 x 711 mm (framed: 1107 x 905 x 105 mm)
Tate Collection. Purchased 1981

Paul Nash 1889-1946
Landscape from a Dream 1936-38
Oil on canvas
679 x 1016 mm (framed: 754 x 883 x 70 mm)
Tate Collection. Presented by The Contemporary Art Society 1946

John Armstrong 1893-1973
Dreaming Head 1938
Tempera on wood
478 x 794 mm (framed: 654 x 966 x 84 mm)
Tate Collection. Purchased 1938

Roland Penrose 1900-1984
Le Grand Jour 1938
Oil on canvas
762 x 1010 mm
Tate Collection. Purchased 1964

Roland Penrose 1900-1984
Magnetic Moths 1938
Mixed media, drawing and watercolour on board
594 x 849 x 23 mm
Tate Collection. Purchased 1976

Roland Penrose 1900-1984
Portrait 1939
Oil on canvas
762 x 637 mm (framed: 805 x 950 x 80 mm)
Tate Collection. Purchased 1982

Conroy Maddox 1912-2005
The Fabled Garden 1939
Gouache
305 x 432 mm
Private Collection

F. E. McWilliam 1902-1992
Eye, Nose and Cheek
Hoptonwood stone
889 x 870 x 266 mm
Tate Collection. Purchased 1966

Humphrey Jennings 1907-1950
The House in the Woods 1939-44
Oil on canvas
432 x 533 mm (framed: 519 x 620 x 43 mm)
Tate Collection. Presented by Mrs Cicely Jennings 1971

Humphrey Jennings 1907-1950
Train (Locomotive 101) 1939-44
Oil on canvas
635 x 1013 mm (framed: 692 x 1073 x 63 mm)
Tate Collection. Presented by the Trustees of the Elephant Trust 1981

F. E. McWilliam 1909-1992
Profile 1940
Wood
622 x 178 mm
Tate Collection. Purchased 1963

Conroy Maddox 1912-2005
The Strange Country 1940
Mixed media and watercolour on paper
406 x 279 mm
Tate Collection. Purchased 1971

Conroy Maddox 1912-2005
The Ceremony 1940
Pencil and gouache on card
229 x 438 mm
The Sammlung Ming, London

Max Ernst 1891-1976
Alice in 1941 1941
Oil on paper mounted on canvas
400 x 323 mm
The Museum of Modern Art, New York. James Thrall Soby Bequest, 1980

Oskar Kokoschka 1886-1980
Anschluss - Alice im Wunderland 1941
Oil on canvas
635 x 736 mm
Private Collection

Dorothea Tanning born 1910
Eine Kleine Nachtmusik 1943
Oil on canvas
407 x 610 mm (framed: 640 x 833 x 85 mm)
Tate Collection. Purchased with assistance from the Art Fund and the
American Fund for the Tate Gallery 1997

Paul Nash 1889-1946
Flight of the Magnolia 1944
Oil on canvas
511 x 762 x 22 mm (framed: 687 x 942 x 85 mm)
Tate Collection. Purchased with assistance from the Friends of the Tate
Gallery, the Art Fund and a group of donors 1999

Salvador Dalí and Walt Disney
Destino 1946 (completed 2003)
Colour, sound
7 minutes
Artwork provided courtesy of Animation Research Library, Walt Disney
Animation Studios, Burbank, California

Salvador Dalí 1904-1989
Four storyboard drawings for the Walt Disney film *Destino* 1946
Pen and ink on paper
203 x 228 mm
Artwork provided courtesy of Animation Research Library, Walt Disney
Animation Studios, Burbank, California

Salvador Dalí 1904-1989
Nude Torso on Checkerboard 1946
Oil on canvas
457 x 610 mm
Artwork provided courtesy of Animation Research Library, Walt Disney
Animation Studios, Burbank, California

Salvador Dalí 1904-1989
Open Field with Ball in Centre 1946
Oil on canvas
510 x 635 mm
Artwork provided courtesy of Animation Research Library, Walt Disney
Animation Studios, Burbank, California

Max Ernst 1832-1898
La Chasse au Snark 1950
Illustrated book
Max Ernst Museum Brühl des LVR, Stiftung Max Ernst

Max Ernst 1891-1976
Pour les amis d'Alice 1957
Oil on canvas
1160 x 900 mm
Courtesy of Fondation Treilles, Tourtour, France

René Magritte 1898-1967
Alice in Wonderland 1957
Film 8mm, black and white
4 minutes
Royal Museums of Fine Arts of Belgium – Archives of Belgian Art
Letters and Documents, Brussels

Max Ernst 1891-1976
Thirty-three Little Girls set out for the White Butterfly Hunt 1958
Oil on canvas
1370 x 1070 mm
Museo Thyssen-Bornemisza, Spain

Robert Smithson 1938-1973
Untitled (Tear) 1961-3
Gouache, photo collage, crayon on paper
609 x 673 mm
The Estate of Robert Smithson, courtesy of James Cohan Gallery, New
York/Shanghai

John Wesley born 1928
Untitled (Falling Alice) 1963
Acrylic on paper
609 x 508 mm
Courtesy of Fredericks & Freiser, New York

John Wesley born 1928
Humpty Dumpty 1963
Acrylic on canvas
609 x 508 mm
Courtesy of Fredericks & Freiser, New York

Joseph Kosuth born 1945
Clock (One and Five), English/Latin Version 1965/1997
Clock, photographs and printed texts
610 x 2902 mm
Tate Collection. Transferred from the Irish Museum of Modern Art
1997

Dorothea Tanning born 1910
Pincushion to Serve as Fetish 1965
Mixed media
372 x 370 x 455 mm
Tate Collection. Purchased 2003

Max Ernst 1832-1898
Logique Sans Peine 1966
Lithographic prints
Max Ernst Museum Brühl des LVR, Stiftung Max Ernst

Adrian Piper born 1948
Alice Down the Rabbit Hole 1966
Oil on canvas
643 x 480 mm
Private Collection, Italy

Adrian Piper born 1948
Alice and the Pack of Cards 1966
Oil on canvas
635 x 480 mm
Private Collection, Italy

Adrian Piper born 1948
The Mad Hatter's Tea Party 1966
Oil on canvas
635 x 480 mm
Private Collection, Italy

Yayoi Kusama born 1929
Alice in Wonderland Happening 1968
Four photographic prints
Each: 230 x 170 mm
Yayoi Kusama

Yayoi Kusama born 1929
Press release from *Alice in Wonderland Happening* 1968
Print on paper (facsimile copy)
275 x 215 mm
Yayoi Kusama

Paul Laffoley born 1940
Alice Pleasance Liddell 1968
Oil, acrylic and ink on canvas
1867 x 1258 x 89 mm
Courtesy of the artist and Kent Fine Art, New York

Jan Dibbets born 1941
Perspective Correction – square with 2 diagonals 1968
Black and white photograph on photographic canvas
1100 x 1100 mm
Private Collection

Salvador Dalí 1904-1989
Alice in Wonderland 1969
Set of twelve illustrations
Each: 600 x 500 mm
Collection of Charlie Lovett, Winston-Salem, N.C., USA

Jan Dibbets born 1941
Perspective Correction – My Studio II, 3: Square with Cross on Floor
1969
Black and white photograph on photographic canvas
1099 x 1102 x 19 mm
Courtesy of Glenstone

Mel Bochner born 1940
Language is not transparent 1969
Ink stamped on graph paper
247 x 178 mm (framed: 446 x 324 mm)
Tate Collection. Presented anonymously 2009

Max Ernst 1832–1898
Alice in Wonderland from Lewis Carroll's Wunderhorn 1970
Lithographic prints
Max Ernst Museum Brühl des LVR, Stiftung Max Ernst

Graham Ovenden born 1943
Alice 1970
Eight screenprints on paper
Each: 242 x 181 mm
Tate Collection. Presented by Rose and Chris Prater through the
Institute of Contemporary Prints 1975

Peter Blake born 1932
from *Illustrations to Through the Looking-Glass* 1970
Eight screenprint on paper
Each: 242 x 180 mm
Tate Collection. Presented by Rose and Chris Prater through the
Institute of Contemporary Prints 1975

Francesca Woodman 1958-1981
Untitled (Boulder, Colorado) 1972-75
Photographic print on paper
325 x 310 mm
Courtesy George and Betty Woodman and Victoria Miro Gallery

Marcel Broodthaers 1924-1976
Literary Paintings. English Series. 1972
Screenprint ink on primed canvas
9 parts, each: 812 x 1011 x 30 mm
Collection of Linda & Guy Pieters

VALIE EXPORT born 1940
Belgian Intersection 1972-73
Black and white photographic collage
850 x 310 x 10 mm
VALIE EXPORT, Strassenkreuzung Belgien, 1972/73, b/w photography,
photocollage, courtesy: Charim Wien/Charim Ungar Berlin

Marcel Broodthaers 1924-1976
Cartes d'Alice in Wonderland 1973
Nineteen projection slides of a 19th century set of playing cards based
on Alice in Wonderland
Dimensions variable
Marie-Puck Broodthaers Gallery

VALIE EXPORT born 1940
Schriftzug Wien - Venedig 1973
Black and white photographic print
500 x 150 x 20 mm
VALIE EXPORT, Schriftzug Wien-Venedig, 1972/73, courtesy Charim
Wien / Charim Ungar Berlin

Marcel Broodthaers 1924-1976
Comédie 1974
Offset print on paper
636 x 456 mm
Marie-Puck Broodthaers Gallery

Marcel Broodthaers 1924-1976
Hôtel du Grand Miroir 1974
Pen on paper
207 x 345 mm (framed: 260 x 345 mm)
Marie-Puck Broodthaers Gallery

Terry Fox 1943-2008
Children's Tapes 1974
Black and white, sound
30 minutes
Electronic Arts Intermix, New York

Duane Michals born 1932
Alice's Mirror 1974
Seven gelatin prints with hand applied text
1270 x 1780 mm
Pace/Macgill Gallery, New York

Francesca Woodman 1958-1981
Untitled (Providence, Rhode Island) 1975-78
Photographic print on paper
325 x 310 mm
Courtesy George and Betty Woodman and Victoria Miro Gallery

Francesca Woodman 1958-1981
Untitled (Providence, Rhode Island) 1975-78
Photographic print on paper
325 x 310 mm
Courtesy George and Betty Woodman and Victoria Miro Gallery

Francesca Woodman 1958-1981
Yet another leaden sky, Rome 1977-78
Photographic print on paper
325 x 310 mm
Courtesy George and Betty Woodman and Victoria Miro Gallery

Francesca Woodman 1958-1981
Untitled 1979-80
325 x 310 mm
Photographic print on paper
Courtesy George and Betty Woodman and Victoria Miro Gallery

Liliana Porter born 1941
The End of the Journey 1980
Photoetching, silkscreen and chine colle
648 x 959 mm
Courtesy of the artist

Liliana Porter born 1941
The Way Out 1983
Silkscreen on paper
648 x 959 mm
Courtesy of the artist

Gary Hill born 1951
Why do things get in a muddle? (Come on Petunia) 1984
Video installation
32 minutes
Courtesy of the artist and Inter Media Art Institute, Dusseldorf

Bill Woodrow born 1948
English Heritage – Humpty Fucking Dumpty 1987
Mixed media
2390 x 3276 x 1067 mm
Tate Collection. Purchased 1987

Liliana Porter born 1941
Sea Side 1989
Mixed media collage on watercolour paper
762 x 559 mm
Courtesy of the artist

Tim Rollins and K.O.S. born 1955
White Alice (After Lewis Carroll) 1989
Acrylic on book mounted on canvas
1828 x 3200 x 38 mm
Jane and Leonard Korman

Rodney Graham born 1949
Alice's Adventures in Wonderland 1989 (2011 exhibition copy)
Tin slipcase
195 x 160 x 28 mm
Courtesy of Yves Gevaert, Anghiari

Anna Gaskell born 1969
Untitled #2 (Wonder) 1996
Chromogenic print
1208 x 1006 mm
Courtesy of the artist and Yvon Lambert, New York

Anna Gaskell born 1969
Untitled #5 (Wonder) 1996
Chromogenic print
1221 x 1022 mm
Courtesy of the artist and Yvon Lambert, New York

Anna Gaskell born 1969
Untitled #8 (Wonder) 1996
Chromogenic print
736 x 895 mm
Courtesy of the artist and Yvon Lambert, New York

Anna Gaskell born 1969
Untitled #6 (Wonder) 1996
Chromogenic print
483 x 590 mm
Courtesy of the artist and Yvon Lambert, New York

Diana Thater born 1962
The Caucus Race 1998
2 LCD-video projectors, 4 video monitors, 6 dvd players,
1 sync-generator, 6 dvds
Dimensions variable
Courtesy of David Zwirner, New York and Hauser & Wirth

Douglas Gordon born 1966
Through a Looking Glass 1999
2 video projections
Dimensions variable
Astrup Fearnley Collection, Oslo, Norway

Dan Graham born 1942
Girl's Make-up Room 1998-2000
Two-way mirror glass, perforated stainless steel, wooden stool and
cosmetic articles
1702 x 2997 mm
Courtesy of Hauser & Wirth and Lisson Gallery

Kiki Smith born 1954
Pool of Tears 2 (after Lewis Carroll) 2000
Intaglio with hand-colouring
1295 x 1873 mm (framed: 1372 x 1999 x 63 mm)
Courtesy of ULAE, Inc.

Fiona Banner born 1966
Arsewoman in Wonderland Act I 2001
Screenprint on paper, two panels
3960 x 2600 mm
Courtesy of the artist

Pierre Huyghe born 1962
A Smile without a Cat 2002
Single channel video, sound
5 minutes 46 seconds
Courtesy of Marian Goodman Gallery, New York & Paris

Kiki Smith born 1954
Come Away From Her (After Lewis Carroll) 2003
Intaglio with hand-colouring
1286 x 1874 mm (framed: 1372 x 1981 x 64 mm)
Courtesy of ULAE, Inc.

Jason Rhoades 1965-2006
Tate Touche from My Madinah: in pursuit of my ermitage 2004
Neon lights, cable, towelling, ribbon, plastic, amethyst crystal and wax
Dimensions variable
Tate Collection. Lent by the American Fund for the Tate Gallery,
courtesy of the American Acquisitions Committee, 2006

Joseph Grigely born 1956
167 White Conversations 2004
Mixed media
1250 x 3685 mm
Tate Collection. Lent by the American Fund for the Tate Gallery,
courtesy of the American Acquisitions Committee, 2005

Nalini Malani born 1946
Alice 2006
Acrylic and enamel reverse painting on mylar
1830 x 820 x 30 mm
Yugo

Samantha Sweeting born 1982
Run Rabbit, Run Rabbit, Run Run Run 2007
Single channel video, silent
2 minutes
Courtesy of the artist

Allen Ruppersberg born 1944
The Never Ending Book 2007
800 photocopies, two banners, 34 sculptural elements
Dimensions variable
Tate Collection. Purchased with funds provided by the American Fund
for the Tate Gallery 2008

Luc Tuymans born 1958
Wonderland 2007
Oil on canvas
3530 x 5470 mm
Courtesy of David Zwirner, New York

Annelies Štrba born 1947
Nyima 405 2009
Archival pigment print on canvas
1100 x 1650 mm
Courtesy of the artist and Frith Street Gallery, London

Annelies Štrba born 1947
Nyima 438 2009
Archival pigment print on canvas
1100 x 1650 mm
Courtesy of the artist and Frith Street Gallery, London

Annelies Štrba born 1947
Nyima 445 2009
Archival pigment print on canvas
1100 x 1650 mm
Courtesy of the artist and Frith Street Gallery, London

AA Bronson born 1946
Through the Looking Glass 2009
Twelve mirrors, each composed of 60 leaves of transparent plastic
Each: 360 x 310 mm
Michèle Didier

Torsten Lauschmann born 1970
Digital Clock (Growing Zeros) 2010
Playback from Macmini, HD Projection
Dimensions variable, duration: 24 hours
Courtesy of the artist; Mary Mary, Glasgow

Yifat Bezalel born 1975
A Broken Hill, Hidud (Echoing), Lovers?, Wild Nobleman and Chasing the Moonlight 2010
Pencil and ink on paper, stickers
Installation of 5 drawings, dimensions variable
Courtesy of the artist and Gowen Contemporary, Geneva

Michelle Stuart born 1938
The Other Side of the Glass 2010
Altered archival inkjet photographs
Diptych, each panel of plates: 635 x 1334 mm (254mm in between)
Michelle Stuart and Leslie Tonkonow Artworks & Projects

Mel Bochner born 1940
Measurement: Perimeter (Ask Alice) 1969/2011
Vinyl tape
Overall display dimensions variable
Courtesy of the artist

Jimmy Robert born 1975
Untitled (the mirror is on stage, performance/installation) 2011
19th century Japanese folding screen with gold leaf, mirrors, paper
1750 x 3600 mm
Courtesy of the artist and Galerie Diana Stigter

Exhibited illustrated editions and adaptations kindly lent by
Edward Wakeling Collection and Richards Collection.

Copyright and photography credits

Artists

John Armstrong
p.102 © Tate
Balthus
p.20 © 2011. Digital Image. The Museum of Modern Art, New York/Scala, Florence
Fiona Banner
pp.156-7 Courtesy of the artist
Alexander Bassano
pp.33 Private Collection, Courtesy of Hans P. Kraus Jr, New York, 79 © National Portrait Gallery, London
Yifat Bezalel
p.163 © Studio Giradet
Sir Peter Blake
pp.138, 139 © Peter Blake 2002. All rights reserved DACS
Sir William Richmond Blake
p.35 Private Collection
Mel Bochner
pp.145, 165 Courtesy of the artist
Marcel Broodthaers
p.142 Linda and Guy Pieters
AA Bronson
p.146 © AA Bronson, 2009, courtesy Esther Schipper
Julia Margaret Cameron
p.32 © National Portrait Gallery, London
Salvador Dali
pp.116, 117 ©Salvador Dali. Fundacio Gala-Salvador Dali, DACS 2011 Images supplied © 2011 Courtesy of the Salvador Dali Museum, St. Petersburg, FL, USA
Salvador Dali and Walt Disney
pp.118, 119 © Disney
Charles L Dodgson
Front Cover, Image from Edward Wakeling Collection
pp.27, 36, 39 (below), 40, 45 (top right; bottom right), 54, 192 Morris L. Parrish Collection, Department of Rare Books and Special Collections, Princeton University Library
pp.26, 28, 30, 31, 44 © National Media Museum/SSPL
pp.29, 41 © National Portrait Gallery, London
p.34 Collection of Charlie Lovett, Winston-Salem, N.C., USA
pp.39 (right; bottom right), 43, 45 (bottom left), 48 Gernsheim Collection, Harry Ransom Humanities Research Center, The University of Texas at Austin
pp.46, 47 © Tate
pp.60, 61, 66 © British Library Board
pp.45 (top left) Courtesy of Edward Wakeling and The Lewis Carroll Society
pp.62, 63, 64, 65, 67, 68, 69, 70 (and 121), 71, 72-73 All images reproduced by kind permission of Christ Church Library and Archive, University of Oxford
Max Ernst
pp.15, 110, 111, 112, 113, 114, 115 (left; right) © ADAGP, Paris and DACS, London 2011 and
p.110 Private Collection Starnberg, Germany
p.111 © 2011 The Museum of Modern Art, New York/Scala, Florence
p.113 © Jacqueline Hyde Ph. et Foundation de Treilles, Tourtour
p.114, 115 (left) Courtesy Max Ernst Museum Bruhl des LVR, Stiftung Max Ernst
p.115 (right) © 2011 The Museum of Modern Art, New York/Scala, Florence
Anna Gaskell
pp.152, 153 Courtesy of the artist, Yvon Lambert
Douglas Gordon
p.172 Photo Stuart Tyson, Taxi Driver © 1976 Columbia Pictures Industries, Inc. All rights reserved. Courtesy Columbia Picture
Emmet Gowin
p.93 © Emmet and Edith Gowin. Courtesy Pace/MacGill Gallery, New York

Dan Graham
p.173 © Courtesy of the artist and Marian Goodman Gallery, New York
Rodney Graham
p.158 Yves Gevaert, Anghiari
Joseph Grigely
pp.170-171 © Joseph Grigely
Mary Heilman
p.21 Courtesy Private Collection, Los Angeles
Gary Hill
p.164 © Gary Hill and IMAI – inter media art institute, Dusseldorf
Arthur Hughes
p.50 © Laing Art Gallery, Newcastle, Tyne and Wear Archives and Museums
p.51 © 2011 AGO
William Holman Hunt
p.52-53 © Tate
Pierre Huyghe
p.169 © Courtesy of the artist and Marian Goodman Gallery, New York
Humphrey Jennings
p.106 © Humphrey Jennings
Oskar Kokoschka
p.109 © Winer Stadtische Versicherung AG Vienna Insurance Group
Joseph Kosuth
pp.126-127 © ARS, NY and DACS, London 2002
Yayoi Kusama
pp. 132, 133 © Yayoi Kusama/Photo by Bob Sabin
Paul Laffoley
p.131 © Courtesy the artist and Kent Fine Art, New York
Torsten Lauschmann
p.127 © Torsten Lauschmann Courtesy of Mary Mary Glasgow
George Dunlop Leslie
p.55 Courtesy The Royal Pavilion & Museums, Brighton and Hove
Conroy Maddox
p.107 © Private Collection
Nalini Malani
p.162 © Nalini Malani
Sally Mann
p.83 © Sally Mann. Courtesy Gagosian Gallery
F E McWilliam
p.105 © The estate of F E McWilliam
Duane Michals
pp.140-141 © Duane Michals. Courtesy Pace/MacGill Gallery, New York
John Everett Millais
p.49 © Perth Museum and Art Gallery, Perth and Kinross Council, Scotland
Paul Nash
pp.98-99 © Tate
Graham Ovenden
pp.136, 137 © Graham Ovenden
Sir Roland Penrose
p.103 © The estate of Sir Roland Penrose
Adrian Piper
pp.134, 135 Courtesy Konrad Baumgartner. Private Collection Milan
Sigmar Polke
p.130 © The Estate of Sigmar Polke/DACS, London 2011
Liliana Porter
p.167 Courtesy of the Artist
Oscar Gustav Rejlander
p.24 Gernsheim Collection, Harry Ransom Humanities Research Center, The University of Texas at Austin
Jason Rhoades
p.168 © The estate of Jason Rhoades
Tim Rollins
pp.150-151 © Courtesy the artist and Lehmann Maupin Gallery.
Allan Ruppersberg
pp.148, 149 © Allan Ruppersberg

Kiki Smith
pp.160, 161 © Courtesy of ULAE, inc
Robert Smithson
p.144 © Estate of Robert Smithson, Courtesy of James Cohan Gallery,
New York/Shanghai, licensed by VAGA, New York
Annalies Strba
pp.176-7 © Courtesy the artist and Frith Street Gallery , London
Michelle Stuart
pp. 174, 175 © Michelle Stuart
Samantha Sweeting
p.90 © Samantha Sweeting. Photo credit: Lisa Newman (filming)
Dorothea Tanning
pp.100, 101 © ADAGP, Paris and DACS, London 2011
John Tenniel
pp.74, 75 © Rosenbach Museum & Library, Philadelphia
Diane Thater
p.166 © Courtesy David Zwirner, New York
Luc Tuymans
pp. 154-5 © Courtesy David Zwirner, New York
Valie Export
p.143 © Valie Export.   Courtesy Charim Galerie Wien Berlin
John Wesley
p.129 © Courtesy Fredericks and Freiser, New York
Francesca Woodman
pp. 91, 93, 147 © Courtesy of George and Betty Woodman and Victoria
Miro Gallery
Bill Woodrow
p.159 © Bill Woodrow

Other images

p.24 (Wet-Collodion Photographic Outfit) © The University of Oxford
for its Museum of the History of Science, 2011
p.24 (Ottewill Box Camera) © National Media Museum/SPPL
pp.76, 77 Courtesy of Edward Wakeling and The Lewis Carroll Society
p.78 © Victoria and Albert Museum, London

With thanks to Edward Wakeling and Christoph Schulz for assistance
in sourcing images.

Disclaimer: Should, despite intensive research any person entitled to
rights have been overlooked, legitimate claims shall be compensated
within the usual provisions.

Sponsors and Donors

The Art Fund
Tom Bloxham MBE
British Council
BT
Business in the Arts: North West
DLA Piper
Eleanor Rathbone Charitable Trust
Embassy of the Kingdom of the Netherlands
European Commission,
    through the Youth in Action Programme
European Regional Development Fund (ERDF)
The Jacqueline Nonkels Fund,
    managed by the King Baudouin Foundation
Liverpool City Council
Liverpool Primary Care Trust
Liverpool & Sefton Health Partnership Ltd
Museums Libraries and Archives Council
National Lottery through Arts Council England
Northwest Regional Development Agency
Tate Liverpool Members
Mr & Mrs Wilbur Ross
Youth Opportunities Fund

Corporate Partners

David M Robinson (Jewellery) Ltd
DLA Piper
DWF
Hill Dickinson
Liverpool Hope University
Liverpool John Moores University
Unilever UK

Corporate Members

Andrew Collinge Ltd
Bruntwood
Cheetham Bell JWT
Deutsche Bank
Fraser Wealth Management
Grant Thornton
Individual Restaurant Company Plc
KPMG
Lime Pictures
Royal Bank of Scotland

Patrons

Elkan Abrahamson
Hilary Banner
Diana Barbour
David Bell
Lady Beverley Bibby
Jo & Tom Bloxham MBE
Helen Burrell
Paul Carroll & Nathalie Bagnall
Jim Davies
Olwen McLaughlin
Barry Owen OBE
Sue & Ian Poole
Anthony Preston

Charles L. Dodgson
The Broad Walk, Oxford, 1857